DEC   2006

At Issue

Is Factory Farming Harming America?

WITHDRAWN
PRINT

Other books in the At Issue series:

At Issue

Is Factory Farming Harming America?

Stuart A. Kallen, Book Editor

GREENHAVEN PRESS

An imprint of Thomson Gale, a part of The Thomson Corporation

THOMSON

GALE

Detroit • New York • San Francisco • New Haven, Conn. • Waterville, Maine • London

Christine Nasso, *Publisher*
Elizabeth Des Chenes, *Managing Editor*

© 2006 Thomson Gale, a part of The Thomson Corporation.

Thomson and Star logo are trademarks and Gale and Greenhaven Press are registered trademarks used herein under license.

For more information, contact:
Greenhaven Press
27500 Drake Rd.
Farmington Hills, MI 48331-3535
Or you can visit our Internet site at http://www.gale.com

LIBRARY OF CONGRESS CATALOGING-IN-PUBLICATION DATA

Is factory farming harming America? / Stuart A. Kallen, book editor.
    p. cm. -- (At issue)
  Includes bibliographical references and index.
  ISBN-13: 978-0-7377-3437-9 (hardcover : alk. paper)
  ISBN-10: 0-7377-3437-X (hardcover : alk. paper)
  ISBN-13: 978-0-7377-3438-6 (pbk. : alk. paper)
  ISBN-10: 0-7377-3438-8 (pbk. : alk. paper)
  1. Livestock factories--United States. 2. Animal industry--United States. I. Kallen,
Stuart A., 1955– II. Series: At issue (San Diego, Calif.)
  SF140.L58I87 2006
  338.1'760973--dc22
                                                        2006020094

Printed in the United States of America
10 9 8 7 6 5 4 3 2 1

Contents

Introduction

In 1973 U.S. Secretary of Agriculture Earl Butz gave American farmers an ultimatum: In their business, Butz predicted, farmers would have to "get big or get out." The secretary's comment was made at a time when unfavorable economic conditions were forcing millions of farmers off the land every year: In 1973 there were about 2.5 million farmers in the United States, down from 20 million only two decades earlier. Unless small farmers could increase their production and cut costs, their numbers were sure to shrink further.

Many farmers who survived into the 1980s "got big" by buying more land, purchasing bigger machinery to farm it, and building bigger facilities to raise more cows, pigs, chickens, turkeys, and other livestock. This kind of expansion was an expensive proposition, however, beyond the financial reach of many family farmers; thus, wealthy corporate conglomerates became the newest farmers in the countryside. For example, in 1970 the oil and natural gas company Tenneco, one of the nation's largest corporations, bought the Kern County Land Company, a California-based food grower that was the oldest and largest agricultural company in the United States. The same year, Tenneco acquired the nation's largest vegetable and fruit distributor. With this purchase Tenneco was able to consolidate control over a major percentage of the food industry. The company's farm machines ran on Tenneco petroleum and grew food with its petroleum-based agricultural chemicals on company land. The harvested food was distributed to the supermarket by another Tenneco company. This control allowed Tenneco to sell food much more cheaply than family farmers could, bound by higher prices for fuel and power, feed and fertilizers, and distribution.

Thousands of independent farmers found they could not compete in an economic environment in which 2 percent of the biggest agricultural companies, like Tenneco, sold more than one-third of all food products in the United States. As Christopher D. Cook writes in *Diet for a Dead Planet*:

> Corporations rarely put farmers out of business in any immediate sense, yet their consolidating control over the entire food industry speeded the demise of the smaller independent farmers by reducing growers' selling options at the front of the market process and reducing their crops to cheap raw inputs for processed retail food. . . . For the most part, corporations weren't interested in farming . . . they were more intent on controlling agribusiness . . . [by] commanding the food industry from farm to dinner table, and dominating near-monopoly markets.

In the 1980s the trend toward large-scale farming continued to accelerate as high interest rates and several economic recessions helped push smaller farmers into financial ruin. Between 1982 and 1987 alone, America lost more than 30,000 farms a year—153,217 in half a decade. Widespread bankruptcy forced land prices down and allowed large corporations to further expand their holdings.

With millions of dollars to invest in their growing agricultural concerns, large corporations hired biologists and other scientists to staff cutting-edge research-and-development programs aimed at improving farming methods and ultimately maximizing profits. Following an agricultural trend that began after World War II, when pesticides, synthetic fertilizers, and advances in livestock production made farming more productive, agribusiness implemented scientific methods to produce food at the lowest possible price. These procedures are now an integral part of what is known as factory farming.

The factory farming model depends on mechanization and economies of scale. To save space and eliminate the need for close supervision, extremely large numbers of farm animals, sometimes several million, are confined in small spaces, ranging from communal pens to individual cages, housed in giant metal buildings, a system called confined animal feeding operations or CAFOs. Because CAFOs increase the risk of bacterial spread, potentially leading to disease epidemics, animals are fed antibiotics along with hormones and vitamins to encourage fast growth. To reduce the high cost of feeding the animals, expensive grains and hay are mixed with lower-cost recycled feed and nontraditional foods such as molasses, beet pulp, cottonseed meal, and even farm waste such as chicken manure. Further alteration of the food chain involved the introduction of genetically engineered varieties of traditional animal feed such as corn and soybeans developed to tolerate pesticides and produce higher yields.

These methods have been very successful: Agribusiness profits have far outpaced small farm profits, and over the past fifteen years factory farms have not only dominated U.S. food production but also changed the rural landscape. In Missouri, for example, a single company, Premium Standard Farms, raises 2.5 million pigs at a time on 37,000 acres and produces 25 percent of all pork in that state. In North Carolina, the pig population quadrupled from 2.5 to 10 million between 1987 and 1997, while a single slaughterhouse owned by Smithfield Foods turns 24,000 hogs into food every day. Although the factory hog farms generate more than $3 billion a year, North Carolina lost about 70 percent of its small pig farms since 1990.

Within the past decade, factory farming has come under scrutiny, and increasing controversy, for its significant effects on traditional farmers, farm animals, and the environment. However, there is little doubt that factory farms produce food that is cheap and plentiful. Americans spend only 10 percent of their income on food, less than people in any other industrialized nation. And, as never before, grocery stores in the United States are crowded with tens of thousands of foods that suit almost any taste.

With gleaming aisles of fresh produce, dairy cases stocked with milk products, freezers filled with processed food, and meat counters offering inexpensive, high quality beef, pork, turkey, and chicken, few consumers think about where their food comes from. Some activists, environmentalists, and researchers hope to change that situation by educating Americans about food produced on factory farms and sounding alarms about adverse health and environmental effects. The contributors to *At Issue: Is Factory Farming Harming America?* debate the necessity for, benefits of, and problems associated with this modern agricultural revolution.

1

Industrial Farming Is Harming Farmers, the Environment, and Public Health

Ronnie Cummins

Ronnie Cummins is the executive director of the Organic Consumers Association, former director of Jeremy Rifkin's Beyond Beef Campaign & Pure Food Campaign, and the coauthor of Genetically Engineered Foods: A Self-Defense Guide for Consumers.

Large-scale, industrial farming has been a been a disaster on nearly every level. Billions of tons of polluting pesticides and fertilizers have destroyed waterways and contributed to global warming. Large corporations have pushed millions of family farmers off the land. And the food produced on factory farms is responsible for causing cancer, food-borne illnesses, and the obesity epidemic sweeping the nation. After poisoning the air, water, and people of the United States for the last sixty years, large agribusiness companies are now exporting the factory farming model to impoverished nations across the globe. American consumers need to support small farmers who grow organic foods and resist the drive by giant corporations to take total control of the world's food production systems.

The last sixty years of "modern" industrial agriculture in the United States, characterized by ever-higher chemical, technology, and energy inputs, can only be characterized as a

Ronnie Cummins, "Fatal Harvest: Sixty Years of Industrial Agriculture," Organic Consumers Association, February 7, 2006. Reproduced by permission.

"Fatal Harvest," for small farmers, the environment, biodiversity, and public health.

This industrialized junk food system has not only polluted the environment, depleted aquifers, destroyed topsoil, and released enormous greenhouse and ozone-depleting gases; but has also engendered an epidemic of obesity, heart disease, and cancer, as well as reproductive and hormone disorders—not to mention 86 million cases of food poisoning a year.

Whether we're looking at the annual impact of 12 billion pounds of chemical nitrate fertilizers; a billion pounds of toxic pesticides, herbicides, and fungicides; thousands of tons of antibiotic residues and hormones in dairy products and meat (80% of all antibiotics produced in the country are added to animals to force the animals to grow faster and to survive the hellish conditions of factory-style farms and intensive confinement); massive applications of industrial waste and sewage sludge on the nation's farmlands, and literally billions of pounds of tainted slaughterhouse waste, blood, fat, and raw manure fed to animals on non-organic farms, it's a wonder we're not all dead.

The total number of farms in the United States has declined from 6.5 million in 1935 to around 2 million in 1997.

Now with the advent of so-called "Free Trade" treaties such as the North American Free Trade Agreement (NAFTA), and the General Agreement on Trade and Tariffs (GATT) of World Trade Organization, this Fatal Harvest of American-style industrial agriculture and genetic engineering is being touted as the preferred model for the entire world.

Even ignoring the health hazards of junk food, genetic engineering, food irradiation, and industrial agriculture for a moment, the likely global environmental and socio-economic consequences of adopting the American-style system of energy and chemical-intensive factory farming and long distance food transportation are apocalyptic.

Few Family Farms Left

Using the USA as a model, let's look at the end results of 60 years of industrial agriculture, of taxpayers being misled or brainwashed into subsidizing corporate farms and industrial production techniques to the tune of $20–40 billion a year, of consuming increasing amounts of cheap convenience food, and of allowing giant wholesale and retail monopolies (Cargill, ADM, Wal-Mart, McDonald's, ConAgra, Kraft, Monsanto) to control the food, seed, and fiber marketplace.

First of all the dynamics of corporate-dominated, energy and chemical-intensive industrial agriculture have driven most of America's family farmers off the land. The total number of farms in the United States has declined from 6.5 million in 1935 to around 2 million in 1997. Most of this decline has taken place among small and medium-sized family farms. Even the small number of farmers remaining today exaggerates how many family farms are left, because most are part-time residential or retirement farms. Recent USDA statistics show that 61% of USA farm production is coming from the nation's largest 161,000 farms (8% of all farms), while only 39% of all production is coming from the remaining 92% of small farms.

The U.S. Bureau of the Census stopped counting "farm residents" in 1993 because there were so few farmers left. In contrast, in 1900, farm residents made up 35 percent of the total population. The average non-organic farmer in the U.S. is 58 years old.

Squeezed by the ever lower prices paid to them by giant agribusiness oligopolies for the food and fiber they produce, and, on the other hand, forced to pay the continually in-creased costs of agricultural inputs (pesticides, fertilizers, seeds, equipment, fuel) to giant chemical and biotech companies, American family farmers are being relentlessly driven off the land.

In order to stay on the land, many of our farmers and ranchers are now forced into poorly paid off-farm employment, which currently provides 90% of the net income they have to meet their survival needs. The only economic "winners" in American agriculture today are large corporate farms; semi-monopolistic grain and commodities traders; seed, biotech, and chemical companies; and giant processors, fast-food restaurants, and supermarket chains. For the rest of rural America, the factory farm, chemical-intensive monoculture cash crop model has proved to be an unmitigated disaster.

Maintaining Control Over The Food Chain

Genetically engineered (GE) crops have simply exacerbated this trend of driving small farms and dairies out of business. The UK-based *Financial Times* has reported that in the U.S., larger farms are planting genetically engineered crops, while smaller farms are more likely to be looking for the GE-free premium price.

Soils are eroding, crop yields in many places are declining, water for irrigation is ever more limited, and drinking water supplies are increasingly contaminated by agricultural runoff.

In his book, *Farmageddon: Food and the Culture of Biotechnology*, Brewster Kneen points out that genetic engineering is just the latest tool in the hands of transnational food giants and chemical companies to maximize their profits while maintaining control over our food chain and those who produce our food and fiber. With cheaper raw materials and multibillion dollar taxpayer subsidies, transnational food corporations can force their way into any market in the world and put their smaller competitors out of business. With the advent of NAFTA since 1994, for instance, Archer Daniels Midland and Cargill have been able to dump hundreds of millions of dollars of taxpayer subsidized corn (six million tons per year) on Mexican markets and drive over a million small indigenous farmers off the land. Similarly the grain giants, export oligopolies, and retail giants (McDonald's, Wal-Mart, etc.) use their control of subsidized crops and animal feeds to dominate the global marketplace and put their competitors out of business. Gene engineers look forward to the same "success" with their herbicide resistant and Bt-spliced GE seeds, helping "more efficient" farmers beat out their inefficient competitors.

Just as chemical fertilizers, toxic pesticides, hybrid seeds, and factory farming were supposed to lead us into the promised land of the Green Revolution after World War Two, today's bioengineers promise to use genetic engineering to feed the world's growing population, solve modern society's food-related health problems, and clean up the mess they've made with chemical-intensive agriculture over the past fifty years.

Even a number of the agrochemical companies now admit that the Green Revolution of chemical-intensive agriculture has not been sustainable. Soils are eroding, crop yields in many places are declining, water for irrigation is ever more limited, and drinking water supplies are increasingly contaminated by agricultural runoff. One billion pounds of toxic pesticides and twelve billion pounds of nitrate chemical fertilizers are being applied to America's farmlands every year, devastating our rural environment. Meanwhile weeds and pests damage or eat up the same proportion of our food crops as they did fifty years ago.

Many of America's rural communities are literal ghost towns. And yet even with this decimation of rural America, the US Department of Agriculture warns that 70% of remaining US family farms are "too small" to be economically viable. As a former USDA Secretary of Agriculture, Earl Butz, told US family farmers, you must "Get big or get out." Apply this model on a global scale, and we're talking about driving approximately two billion "inefficient" small farmers and rural villagers off the land. But where will these displaced farmers and their families go? And what will they do for work?

Looking at North America, more and more family farmers and ranchers are indeed "getting out," selling their land to corporate agribusiness operations or land developers, and retiring. This is hardly surprising given that the giant wholesalers and buyers of US farm products (Cargill, ADM, Wal-Mart, McDonald's, Tyson's, Kraft) are unwilling to pay farmers a fair price, or even pay them money enough to meet the costs of production. Corn for example costs non-organic North American farmers approximately $3.40 to produce a bushel (59 pounds) of corn, while monopoly buyers, such as ADM and Cargill, are generally unwilling to pay more than $2.40 a bushel, with US taxpayers picking up the difference.

Industrial corn provides a case study of what's wrong with American agriculture. As [author] Michael Pollan and others have pointed out, energy-intensive, corporate-controlled, taxpayer-subsidized, pesticide-intensive, and now genetically engineered corn is an unmitigated disaster for the environment, family farmers and public health.

America's industrial-style farms are the number one source of water pollution in the country, routinely contaminating surface waters, municipal water supplies, and aquifers.

Environmental Destruction and Public Health Threats

America's industrial-style farms are the number one source of water pollution in the country, routinely contaminating surface waters, municipal water supplies, and aquifers with billions of pounds of chemical fertilizer runoff, pesticides, and animal manure every year. Fish, frogs, and other creatures that depend upon clean water and wetlands are slowly being exterminated, while consumers are turning more and more to bottled water to avoid contaminated tap water. In terms of the energy crisis, climate disruption and destroying the protective ozone layer, America's energy and chemical intensive farms and long-distance food transportation not only use up enormous amounts of non-renewable fossil fuel, pollute the air, and destroy the ozone layer with pesticides such as methyl bromide, but generate up to 20–25% of climate disrupting greenhouse gases as well. In addition non-organic farms are depleting the topsoil at an alarming rate. Factory farm meat production is a major factor in this environmental devastation, in part because feeding grain to farm animals to produce meat—instead of feeding it directly to humans—involves an unsustainable amount of land, as well as a large loss of energy. It takes 10–20 times as much land to feed people meat as it does to feed them with grain. The routine use of antibiotics in animal feed, residues of which are ingested by humans in every bite of non-organic meat or portion of non-organic dairy, helps to create germs which are antibiotic resistant, thereby threatening the effectiveness of antibiotics in medical use. In addition the over-consumption of meat and dairy products are implicated in many of the chronic degenerative diseases that afflict industrial and newly industrializing societies, particularly heart disease and cancer. The pesticides and herbicides used heavily in industrial agriculture are linked with elevated cancer risks for farm workers and consumers and are coming under greater criticism for their links to hormonal and reproductive disorders. Moreover, chemicals, artificial sweeteners and preservatives, added to modern processed foods, are linked to an epidemic of food allergies, food sensitivities, hyperactivity, and a range of learning and behavior disabilities in children.

In addition, feeding blood, slaughterhouse waste, tainted fat, and animal manure to animals has led to the spread of fatal brain-wasting diseases to humans (Mad Cow Disease). And finally due to the industrialization, filth, and inhuman speed of massive slaughterhouses, added to the disease rampant on factory farms, the bulk of non-organic beef, poultry, turkey, and pork coming out of America's slaughterhouses and processing plants is riddled with dangerous pathogens including e-coli 0157H, salmonella, campylobachter, and listeria. Even the USDA has recommended that all US beef be irradiated, and that American consumers treat their cutting boards and kitchen surfaces as bio-hazard zones. No wonder more and more U.S. consumers are turning to organic food. . . .

Two billion small farmers will be driven off the land, the environment and climate stability will be destroyed, and public health will continue to deteriorate.

The Solution Is in Organic Farming

Third world farmers are threatened by dumping, Free Trade agreements, and genetically engineered crops in the same way that U.S. farmers are. In fact, genetically engineered crops and treaties like NAFTA and GATT are instruments to expand the failed U.S. farm policy around the world. Specifically, genetically engineered and industrial agriculture crops are all about monoculture, producing cash crops for export and the so-called open market, which is actually controlled in every sector, by a handful of giant corporations, who drive down the prices paid to farmers and dump the surplus on the developing world. Industrial agriculture is not about growing a diverse set of crops to feed yourself, neighbors, and local communities. But non-industrial, organic farming is exactly this kind of sustainable farming that is needed to support and maintain the 40% of the world's population who are farmers or rural villagers.

The economic, health, and social damage created by industrial agriculture, corporate globalization, the patenting and gene-splicing of transgenic plants and food-producing animals, is inexorably leading to universal "bioserfdom" in which two billion small farmers will be driven off the land, the environment and climate stability will be destroyed, and public health will continue to deteriorate.

The only solution to this Fatal Harvest is to make organic farming once again the dominant force in agriculture (as it has been for most of the last 10,000 years), to make healthy organic foods and lifestyles the norm, and to restructure global agriculture and commerce so that local and regional production for local and regional markets . . . become the dominant paradigm. And most importantly we must quickly begin to address the global energy crisis (at the root of the wars and conflict in the Middle East) and stabilize the global climate crisis, through drastic greenhouse gas reduction and a global conversion to renewable forms of energy in the agriculture, transportation, and utilities sectors.

2

Commercial Fertilizers and Farms Are Far Superior to Organic Farms

R.I. Throckmorton

R.I. Throckmorton is a soil scientist and former dean of the Kansas State University College of Agriculture in Manhattan, Kansas.

Proponents of organic farming claim that chemical fertilizers are harmful to human health and the environment. Nothing could be further from the truth. Commercial fertilizers improve harvest yields, increase the nutritional value of foods, and allow farmers to grow a wide variety of crops on marginal soils. Without chemical fertilizers, American farmers could not produce enough food to feed the world. While advocates of organic farming preach against the chemical fertilizer industry, their doctrine is unsound, unscientific, and dangerous.

In recent years there has grown up in this country a cult of misguided people who call themselves "organic farmers" and who would—if they could—destroy the chemical fertilizer industry on which so much of our agriculture depends.

These so-called organic farmers preach a strange, two-pronged doctrine compounded mainly of pure superstition and myth, with just enough half-truth, pseudo science and emotion thrown in to make their statements sound plausible to the uninformed.

R.I. Throckmorton, "The Organic Farming Myths," biblelife.org, 2005. Reproduced by permission.

One prong of their doctrine is a ruthless attack on chemical fertilizers, based on the preposterous supposition that such commercial plant foods "poison" the soil, destroy beneficial soil organisms such as earthworms, make crops more susceptible to attacks by insects and diseases, encourage weeds, and damage the health of livestock and humans who eat the crops so fertilized. It has been darkly hinted by the apostles of this organic farming creed that such things as decayed teeth, cancer, apoplexy and cirrhosis of the liver trace back to farmers' use of chemicals.

Men who have appropriated use of the word organic are saying that all soil scientists are wrong and that they are right.

The positive side of their ridiculous dogma is a flat claim that organic matter alone is the answer to better crops and improved nutrition. All you have to do to grow perfect crops, insist these faddists, is to follow certain rituals involving composts and otherwise using organic matter in the soil. Such "organically farmed" crops are supposed to yield more, to be free of insects and diseases, and to have wonderful health-giving qualities for the animals or humans who consume them. If this were true, it would be impossible for us to produce our food requirements, because all of the manure, leaves, twigs grass clippings and crop residues available would fall far short of meeting the need.

In other words, these men who have appropriated use of the word organic are saying that all soil scientists are wrong and that they are right. They are, in effect, saying that farmers are wrong in using almost 20 million tons of commercial fertilizers a year. They are asking that painstaking research results of many generations be cast aside. These cultists apparently believe that by a play on words such as "natural", "chemical" and "organic", they have the key to an immortal truth. Strange as it may seem, those who attack the use of fertilizers have little or no reason to use them, as they usually aren't making their living by farming. Many of them are folks who garden or farm for recreation.

Now, superstitions about soils and fads in nutrition aren't new. They come and go. At first, when questions began coming to me about this one, I wasn't disturbed. But as they persisted and the antifertilizer crusade mounted, I began to fear that such misinformation could damage the status of important agricultural research. One uninformed writer said in a letter that the experiment stations were so heavily subsidized by the fertilizer industry that research workers were not free to tell the truth. Nothing could be farther from the truth, and such statements should not go unchallenged.

What is behind the broad pro and con claims of the organic farmer? The answer is simple and provable: Bunk.

Twisting The Meaning of "Organic"

Let's clear up one point now. This cult has sought to appropriate a good word, "organic", and has twisted its meaning to cover a whole crazy doctrine. The facts are that organic matter in its true sense is an important component of the soil—but soil fertility and the kind of crops you grow on a soil are not determined by humus alone. Soil fertility is determined by the amount of active organic matter, the amount of available mineral nutrients, the activities of soil organisms, chemical activities in the soil solution and the physical condition of the soil.

Any plant foods, whether from organic matter, or from a bag of commercial fertilizer, necessarily came from Nature in the first place.

Ever since we have had soil scientists, they have recognized the values of organic matter. The loss of soil humus through cultivation has long been a matter of concern. So the faddists have nothing new to offer on that score. Organic matter is often called "the life of the soil" because it supplies most of the food needs of the soil organisms which aid in changing non-available plant food materials into forms that are available to the plants, and contains small quantities of practically all plant nutrients. It also is a soil conditioner, bringing about beneficial chemical and physical changes. It has a tremendous influence on the tilth of the soil, and on ability of soil to absorb and retain water.

The chemical role of organic matter is particularly important, as it is the storehouse for the reserve nitrogen supply. When soil nitrogen is not combined with organic matter it can be lost rapidly by leaching. Considerable phosphorus and small quantities of practically all other mineral elements in the soil are made available via the organic matter.

The antichemical-fertilizer doctrine makes a great point of the fact that plant food in organic matter is in "natural" form, while in chemical fertilizer it is "unnatural" and thus supposedly is harmful, if not downright poisonous. The logic of this escapes me. Science completely disproved the conclusion. The facts are that any plant foods, whether from organic matter, or from a bag of commercial fertilizer, necessarily came from Nature in the first place. Why is one more "natural" than another? A plant takes in a given nutrient in the same chemical form whether it came from organic matter, or from a bag of commercial fertilizer. The facts are that practically all plant-food elements carried by organic matter are not used in their organic form; they are changed by microorganisms to the simple chemical forms which the plants can use—the same form in which these elements become available to plants when applied as chemical fertilizers. For example, it is foolish to say that nitrogen in commercial fertilizer is "poisonous" while nitrogen from organic matter is beneficial. The basic nitrogen is the same in either case.

Benefits of Chemical Fertilizers

Although soil organic matter is important, it falls short of solving all soil-fertility needs. If we depended on it alone, our high yields would be out of the question. For example, muck soils [untreated rich, black dirt] contain as much as 20 to 50 per cent organic matter. According to the faddists' theories, you could do little to improve such soils. But they actually need fertilizer for efficient production. J. F. Davis, Michigan State College researcher, found in tests that the yield of wheat on unfertilized muck soils was 5.7 bushels an acre, while the yield on plots receiving the chemical phosphorus and potash was 29.2 bushels per acre. The yield of potatoes was increased from 97 bushels an acre with no treatment, to 697 with commercial fertilizer carrying phosphorus and potash. Cabbage yields were boosted by the same means from 1/2 ton to 27 tons.

Since soil and plant research began, scientists have been investigating the kinds of foods plants need and the forms in which they use them. It is known that at least 14 elements are vital to plant growth. Some such as carbon, hydrogen and oxygen are taken from the air by the plant's chemistry. The plant gets from the soil solution such others as nitrogen, phosphorus, potassium, calcium, magnesium, manganese, copper, zinc, sulphur, iron and boron. Nature, the primary source of them all, hasn't distributed these plant foods through all soils in the amounts or mixtures required to get maximum production. Heavy cropping may take so much out of certain soils that deficiencies of some elements occur. It should be evident that the supply of these elements in a soil cannot be increased by raising crops and turning them under. The plant cannot manufacture them. Thus, when a soil is deficient, the most practical remedy is to apply the right kind of fertilizer.

Nitrogen, of course, is somewhat different. Certain organisms associated with legumes, such as alfalfa and clover, can extract this element from the air. When these legumes are grown and plowed under, the nitrogen in the soil may be increased. However, on most soils in the eastern half of the U.S. it is necessary to supply chemical plant foods, such as lime, phosphorus and potassium and to inoculate the seed, in order to produce successfully these nitrogen-fixing crops. It is an interesting side light that the nitrogen returned to the soil in this "natural" form by legumes, comes from the air; so does the nitrogen in certain kinds of chemical fertilizers. Learning to extract nitrogen from the air has given us unlimited potential supplies of the vital plant food.

Fertilizers produced chemically are not poisons and, therefore cannot poison the soil or the plant's produce.

Chemicals Increase Nutritive Value of Food

Fertilizers produced chemically are not poisons and, therefore cannot poison the soil or the plant's produce. There is no evidence that mineral fertilizers, when applied at recommended rates, are injurious to soils, or that crops produced by the use of such materials are harmful to man or beast. On the contrary, there is much scientific proof that the use of commercial fertilizers on deficient soils will increase the crops' nutritive value.

Protein, important in building living tissue, is increased in corn, for example, by nitrogen fertilizers. Ralph W. Cummings, a director of research at North Carolina State College [says], "The protein content of corn grain grown with fertilizers containing synthetic nitrogen salts, has shown an increase over the unfertilized under practically all conditions." In a large number of experiments, the protein content was increased approximately 3 per cent, that is, where the unfertilized corn had only 5.7 per cent protein, the fertilized averaged 10.4 per cent protein. "It is considered that such higher-protein corn is superior feed-stuff," Cummings reported.

There is no evidence whatever to indicate that chemically fertilized plants are less nutritious than non-fertilized. Director W. M. Fifield of the Florida Experiment Station has said: "Not a single instance has been called to our attention where the use of chemicals in production or protection of our state's crops or livestock has resulted in harmful effects on humans who have consumed them."

If commercial fertilizers did poison the soil, one would expect their continued use to result in a material reduction in crop yields. This, however, has decidedly never been the case. These fertilizers have pointed the way to steadily increased yields of higher quality, more nutritious crops. At the Rothamsted Experiment Station, Harpenden, England, is an experiment with wheat which now has been running more than 100 years. One plot has received nothing but manure, applied at the rate of 14 tons per acre annually. Another has received nothing but chemical fertilizer. Despite the exceptionally heavy manure treatment, the average yield of the manure plot and the chemically fertilized plot has been about the same according to the last records available.

There is nothing to substantiate the claims of the organic-farming cult.

And while organic matter is particularly important in the soil in everyday farming, it has been proved that crops can be grown without soil, without any organic matter whatever, simply by supplying the plants with solutions containing the necessary nutrients in chemical form. In many tests various crops have been grown in pure glass sand—the sand providing only mechanical anchorage for the plant—by feeding solutions which contain the needed elements. This process is beyond the experimental stage. It has been applied to some extent commercially, and our military services have made use of this knowledge of the chemical requirements of plants to grow fresh vegetables for troops in areas where standard methods of farming are not feasible.

Not Harmful to Insects

The claim of the antifertilizer cult that insects and diseases tend to ignore crops grown their "natural" way, and concentrate on chemically fertilized crops, I leave to your imagination. No reputable scientist has yet reported any such observation. But H.E. Myers, head, department of agronomy, Kansas State College, observed [in 2005] on an experimental field in Southern Kansas that green bugs were exceedingly numerous on non-fertilized wheat, while only a few were present on adjoining wheat receiving nitrogen and phosphorus as chemical fertilizers.

The indictment that mineral fertilizers destroy earthworms and beneficial soil bacteria is without foundation. At the Rothamsted Experimental Station, it has been found that earthworms are just as numerous in the soil of the fertilized plots as in the unfertilized—but those in the fertilized area are larger and fatter. Many experiments in this country show that application of superphosphate to soils at rates commonly recommended will increase the population of beneficial soil bacteria. The use of mineral fertilizer will, in general, result in an increase of the organic matter of the soil and thus promote bacteria and earthworms. Organic matter is, of course, a by-product of plant growth; one of the quickest ways to increase it in a soil is to use chemical fertilizer to grow luxuriant green manure crops that will be turned back in the soil, or heavy crops that will leave a large residue of organic material. Without the use of chemical fertilizer it is impossible on some soils to grow legumes that are so essential to good soil management in humid sections. On the gray silt loam soils of Southeastern Kansas, farmers could not grow alfalfa successfully, even though they used large quantities of manure. Fertility experiments on these soils showed that over a 24-year period, the average annual yield of alfalfa on untreated land was only .59, of a ton per acre, while the addition of lime and super-phosphate enabled the land to produce an average yield of 2.29, tons. On this land the lime and superphosphate treat-ment increased the average yield of wheat from 14.6 bushels per acre to 26.3 bushels. Although the purely organic manure was beneficial on these soils, manure alone could not solve the problem of a definite lack of lime and phosphorus.

To sum it up, there is nothing to substantiate the claims of the organic-farming cult. Mineral fertilizers, lime and organic matter all are essential in a sound fertility program. Chemical fertilizers stand between us and hunger.

3

Factory Farm Animals Are Treated Inhumanely

Mark H. Bernstein

Mark H. Bernstein is a professor of philosophy at the University of Texas, San Antonio, and the author of two books on morals and ethics.

From the moment they are born, farm animals are treated in a manner that is inhumane and unethical. Animals are genetically manipulated and fed a dizzying array of dangerous antibiotics, hormones, and other substances so that they will produce as much meat, milk, or eggs as possible. When the animals are sent to slaughterhouses, they are systematically abused by sadistic workers, maimed by machinery, and killed with torturous inefficiency. Those that survive this process are skinned and disemboweled while still alive. This process of factory farming is a true holocaust that consumes hundreds of millions of animals every year. Consumers of meat need to examine the methods by which their food is produced and should feel morally obligated to demand humane treatment for innocent farm animals.

Understanding what happens to animals before we bite into a steak, taste some pork, or munch some chicken is not pleasant. Still, it must be done, for it will show just how much gratuitous pain and suffering we inflict on innocent creatures. . . . We are morally obligated to end all our factory (intensive) farming. Since factory farms produce some 95 percent of the flesh we consume, fulfilling our ethical obligations will call for drastically changing how we live our lives. . . .

Beef Cattle

Of all the farm animals, beef cattle probably lead the best lives. Unfortunately, this does not mean that their lives are good. Although allowed to roam and enjoy some semblance of freedom, beef cattle, like all other intensively farmed animals, are treated purely as a means to an end. The beef cow (I use the term generally to refer to cattle of either sex) is seen as an instrument to maximize the production of meat (and some by-products) with minimal cost. As always, economic considerations dictate the treatment of the animal.

They feed the cattle anything from blood to manure to chicken waste—a significant divergence from the cow's natural diet of grasses.

There are three major stresses that face a beef cow: branding, dehorning, and (for males) castration. Until 1995 there were no federal regulations against face branding. It is difficult to imagine how much pain a fully conscious cow feels when someone firmly presses a scalding-hot branding iron against its face. The body branding now currently in vogue for livestock is somewhat less painful, because the body has fewer nerve cells than the face, but it is still an extremely painful and terrifying experience for the cow. Typically branding and castration are done at the same time. Workers on horseback rope the calves and pin them to the ground. One worker rips the scrotum with a knife while another tears out the calf's testicles. A third simultaneously brands the calf. Its shrieks and frenetic movements inarguably show the suffering that the young calf endures. Dehorning is performed either by a paste that dissolves the horn or by workers who saw it off. We should not be misled into thinking that this is a painless operation. The horn contains many nerve cells, so that pain is virtually a certainty. Usually neither branding, castration, nor dehorning is accompanied by anesthesia.

The knocker. . . has the task of killing the cow using a compressed-air gun that projects a steel bolt into a small area on the cow's forehead.

Growers seek to fatten the beef cow as much as possible at the lowest possible cost. To this end, they feed the cattle anything from blood to manure to chicken waste—a significant divergence from the cow's natural diet of grasses. When the beef cow is heavy enough for slaughter, he is urged onto a truck for transport to the slaughterhouse. Some forty to fifty cows may be crammed into a truck that travels some 1,500 miles. Heat exhaustion commonly ensues in the summer, when temperatures often reach well into the nineties. Cows become too weak to stand, and those who don't die from heat exhaustion may be trampled by other cows weighing in excess of 900 pounds. The animals fare no better in the winter, however. They travel in open trucks at some fifty-five miles per hour in a season when subzero temperatures are common throughout much of the United States and Canada; the wind-chill factor may plummet to fifty degrees below zero. The cows urinate and defecate in the trucks, and the waste quickly freezes in such frigid conditions. This, too, can cause the cows to fall, allowing them to be either severely injured or trampled to death by their truckmates. Be it from great heat or great cold, a cow who falls and is trampled for perhaps ten or fifteen hours endures a harrowing plight. In either case, many are severely injured by the time they reach the slaughterhouse, only to be chained and dragged to the kill area so they can be slaughtered.

The Cow Slaughterhouse

The federal Humane Slaughter Act dictates how cows are to be slaughtered. This affects the approximately 40 million cows that are slaughtered in the United States each year. Workers begin the procedure by ushering the cows into a "knocking box" or to a conveyor-restrainer that carries them to a stun operator. The knocker, usually called a "stunner," has the task of killing the cow using a compressed-air gun that projects a steel bolt into a small area on the cow's forehead. If the gun shoots the bolt powerfully enough and the stunner hits the appropriate spot, the cow is killed or at least rendered unconscious. The bolt is then retracted so that it can be used for the next cow in line.

The stunned cow then passes to the shackler, who wraps a chain around one of its legs. After being shackled, the cow is automatically hoisted to an overhead rail. The cow, now upside down and hanging from one leg, is next met by the "sticker," who cuts the carotid arteries and jugular vein in the cow's neck. In the vernacular, the sticker slits the dead or unconscious cow's throat.

The cow is then allowed a few minutes to bleed out, emptying its blood into a pit below the overhead rail. The dead carcass is next met by workers who skin its head and cut off its head and legs. Further down this (dis)assembly line, the cow has its remaining skin removed, is eviscerated, and cut in half vertically.

Slaughterhouse workers have claimed that 25 percent of the cows were conscious while being shackled and hoisted at their plants.

This scenario, unappetizing as it may be for most of us, describes what *ought* to happen according to federal law. What commonly *does* happen is at odds with these guidelines. Almost anything that can go awry in this process does.

Many problems result from the speed of the entire operation. Large slaughterhouses can slaughter over three thousand cows daily. The stunner is often too hurried to hit the correct spot on the cow's skull. Any of several possible results can ensue. Sometimes the cow escapes from the chute and runs wild in the plant. More frequently the stunner simply tries again. It may take anywhere from four to ten or more blows of the steel bolt before the cow is knocked out or killed. Sometimes the cow is stunned but not knocked out. In this case a dazed but conscious cow is shackled and hoisted on the overhead rail. The frantic cow bellows and stretches in all directions while enduring unimaginable pain. This is not a rare occurrence. Some former slaughterhouse workers have claimed that 25 percent of the cows were conscious while being shackled and hoisted at their plants.

Stickers who meet one of these writhing cows seldom get a "good stick." That is, the cow's arteries and veins are not properly cut to allow the blood to drain. Still, there is no stopping the line, and the cow is next greeted by the head skinners, who literally skin the cow alive. There are times, that is, when a conscious cow has its skin taken off. Sometimes a skinner dealing with this situation will stick a knife in the back of the cow's head to sever the spinal cord, but this only paralyzes the cow from the head down. The cow is still conscious. So even if the skinner cuts the spinal cord, the cow will still be conscious when skinned. Some leggers (those who remove the legs of the cow when it is skinned) have reported that virtually *all* the cows at their facilities were conscious when the removal took place. There have been reports of incidents where a cow was not rendered unconscious until ten minutes after it was improperly stunned. . . .

Hogs

As with the cow, the hog or pig has fallen prey to huge farms owned by powerful corporate interests. Lowering labor costs saves money. These farms employ few workers, each of whom spends little time with any individual hog. Thus, as with cattle, injuries and illnesses can fester and worsen before an employee notices a hog's deteriorated condition. According to some estimates, the average hog receives twelve minutes of human care during its entire life. . . .

A four-hundred-pound pig is forced to live her life in [a] two-foot-wide crate.

Economic considerations demand that pig sheds house as many pigs as possible in the most labor-efficient way. To accomplish this goal, farmers use concrete slats for the hog's floor. Concrete is easy to wash down, and the angled floors allow the excrement to fall down into a collection area. Since any straw would fall through the slats as well, the floor is left virtually bare. The hogs are forced to sleep directly on concrete, even though studies have shown that straw bedding enhances a pig's physical and psychological welfare. Concrete floors bring more than just discomfort, however. Joints swell, skin abrades, and feet get infected. This increases pain and frustration, which in turn lead to internecine fighting.

The poor-quality air that surrounds pigs their entire lives causes respiratory diseases. High levels of air-borne urea and ammonia leave as many as 70 percent of hogs with pneumonia at the time of their slaughter. Simply ventilating these houses by pumping fresh air from the outside has been deemed too expensive. It is cheaper to let some hogs die before reaching the slaughterhouse than to provide them with breathable air.

If allowed, pregnant pigs give birth by building nests that will house as many as ten piglets. The sow expends significant time and energy in picking the proper location and bedding material. In the artificial surroundings of the factory, however, the sow spends her pregnancy in a small crate inside the shed.

In addition to frustrating her natural instincts, the crate endangers the newborn piglets, for the mother can suffocate them merely by turning slightly. Even after pregnancy, the sow is denied any freedom. Farmers find it cheaper to house the sow in a small crate for virtually her entire life; a four-hundred-pound pig is forced to live her life in [a] two-foot-wide crate. The hog cannot turn around, let alone walk or play. These intelligent and psychologically complex animals manifest their frustration by launching themselves against their crates and fighting among themselves, including biting each other's tails. Although free-roaming pigs occasionally fight, tail biting rarely occurs. This activity seems to result from the pigs' extremely confined living spaces. Farmers solve the problem simply by cutting off the piglets' tails. No anesthesia is used. As always, the motivation for all this is economic. The smaller the "homes" are, the more pigs a shed can hold. Moreover, confinement lowers feed costs. Restrained pigs spend less energy, so that less food is required to maintain and fatten them.

The piglets who fail to grow rapidly enough—the runts of the litter—have no value, because uniform size is very important to meat packers. Workers separate these runts from the rest and "thump" them. That is, the workers pick them up by their hind legs and smash their heads against the concrete floor. Those unfortunate enough to survive the first thumping must endure a second one. Some piglets surviving a thumping have their throats stepped on until they die. In a single plant over one hundred piglets can suffer this fate in one day. Here, economic concerns may partner with sadism.

Factory farm pigs lead immensely depressing lives. Soon after birth their ears are clipped for identification purposes, their needle teeth are removed to prevent injuries in fights, and males are castrated (all without anaesthetic); some four months later they are slaughtered. Throughout it all they experience only unrelenting frustration, pain, and suffering. Pigs live in hierarchically structured groups. Some are dominant, some are submissive, and this order emerges only after they spend time together. Adding new pigs to the mix destroys the social structure and almost inevitably leads to vicious fighting. Because their confined areas leave no room for the more submissive or weaker pigs to retreat, these fights produce numerous fatalities. Frequently these battles occur when pigs are transported or awaiting slaughter. . . .

Workers use violence to badger these hogs, which are kicked, whipped, and beaten with almost any imaginable object.

The Hog Slaughterhouse

About 100 million hogs are slaughtered annually in the United States. The prescribed method of slaughter is slightly different from that required by the regulations that putatively govern the slaughter of cows. Hogs are "urged" through a narrow angled restrainer and then electrically (rather than mechanically) stunned. Electrodes held at the rear of the pig's head and back for about 3 seconds ostensibly render it unconscious, if not dead. Then, in a step similar to one in cow slaughterhouses, they are shackled by one leg and hoisted onto an overhead rail. They then have their throats slit and bleed out. Next they are lowered into scalding water, after which they are eviscerated. Problems occur with great frequency everywhere along the production line.

The priority that plant managers place on speed again causes much of the unnecessary pain and suffering. At larger plants a hog is slaughtered every four seconds. Problems occur from the beginning, the chute leading up to the restrainer. Usually two or three men urge the hogs through. Unsurprisingly, many of the hogs are reluctant. They smell the blood, sense the terror, and frantically twist and turn, attempting to escape the chutes; some become crippled. Workers use violence to badger these hogs, which are kicked, whipped, and beaten with almost any imaginable object. Prods are shoved up their rectums. Meat hooks are stuck in their anuses and then pulled. Anything goes, as long as it speeds the hogs to the restrainer. A hog that cannot walk is beaten to death, shoved to the side, and hung up later.

The stunning operation tends to be farcical. The hogs are frenzied when they enter the restrainer—facing every which way, running with fear, and banging into one another. It is not surprising that the stunner often fails to solidly stun them. There are several causes for this. Sometimes hogs come by one on top of another, and the stunner doesn't see the bottom hog. Some stunners enjoy harassing the shackler, so they intentionally misstun the hog to make the shackler's job more difficult. Sometimes they doze off, letting live hogs pass by. Probably the major cause for unsatisfactory stunning, however, derives from orders of the manager.

Plant managers are notorious for requiring the stunners to use low voltage, because high voltage can tear up the meat. The diminished voltage can stun some of the pigs, but it often fails to stun a good size sow or boar. These larger hogs need to be multiply stunned, and even then they may still be conscious when they are shackled, hoisted, and stuck. Plant managers are fully aware that an improperly stunned hog may free himself from the overhead rail after being shackled. In fact, slaughterhouses address such escape attempts by incorporating pens below the overhead rail. These pens are usually small, large enough to hold perhaps two pigs. Sometimes, however, upward of ten or fifteen hogs—all of whom are thoroughly dazed and in excruciating pain—are crammed into the pen. Ostensibly the overhead rail is stopped when hogs fall into the pen, and a worker stuns the penned pigs with a portable stunner. When this task is completed, the hogs are to be reshackled, rehoisted, and stuck before the chain is restarted.

Shacklers often mercilessly beat the penned hogs with lead pipes until the animal is so dazed that he can be reshackled and hoisted. If there are many hogs in the pen, there may not be enough time to beat them. The shackler may chain and hoist an obviously conscious hog. Even those hogs that have been beaten often regain consciousness soon after they find themselves strung up on the overhead rail.

After having their throats slit, the hogs are dropped into scalding (140° F) water to remove their hair. But frequently live hogs are dropped into the water. Usually this is because a hog will tighten its muscles after having its throat slit, instinctively trying to keep the blood in its body. If the hog has not yet bled out or the sticking was performed less than adequately, the hog may be conscious when it hits the water. Sometimes live hogs are dunked into the scalding water because they haven't been stuck *at all*. The speed of the operation may make it impossible for the sticker to slit the throat of every hog that passes through. And sometimes hogs are chased into the scalding tank because some employees find it entertaining. Hogs scream from pain, thrash in the scalding water, and inevitably succumb and drown. This may take a couple of minutes. Plant managers are apt to get angry when a live hog is killed in the scalding tank, but not because of empathy; they realize that a meat inspector is likely to condemn the meat, so that the operation will lose money. The solution is to demand that the workers stick the living hogs and then proceed as usual.

Sadly, although I know of no statistics on the matter, some stunners are mean-spirited and sadistic. I have already mentioned how stunners harass shacklers by sending them conscious animals. There are reports of stunners moving the electric wand from the hog's head to his back without holding it for the required three seconds. Apparently some of the stunners receive perverted pleasure from seeing the hog jump and squeal from the pain. Stickers have also been known to beat hogs mercilessly with lead pipes, puncture their eyes, and cut off their noses. Stickers become annoyed at needing to stick conscious hogs, and the hogs become the innocent victims of their frustration. Also, continuously killing hogs every day may become a bit boring. Novel ways of causing pain, suffering, and death may spice up the day.

As it does with cows, transportation brings torture and death to hogs. Hogs packed into trucks are prone to heat exhaustion in the summertime. They may travel over a thousand miles and not be sprayed down for the entire trip. In the winter they die from the cold. Some, both the dead and the living, freeze to the steel railings of the truck. Workers then toss a cable around them to pull them off the truck and bring them to the slaughterhouse. That a leg may still be attached to the truck after the hog is dragged out is of no concern. At other times, workers use knives or wires to pry the hogs loose. That some of their skin is left on the truck is again of no moment. Since frozen hogs are valueless to the processing plant, they are usually left by the side of the facility. The living receive no care or attention. They are left to fend for themselves and soon die from exhaustion. The nominal power of the Humane Slaughter Act apparently does not apply to frozen hogs. Inspectors make no antemortem examinations, nor are there any regulations to guide their disposal. With frozen hogs—sometimes as many as fifteen or twenty in a truckload—there is not even the pretense of any concern for the animals' welfare.

Overcrowding kills some hogs but constrains costs by letting producers use fewer trucks, fewer drivers, and less fuel. As with cows, moreover, everyone in the chain of command has good reason to neither report nor correct inhumane practices. And so it goes, while the pigs pay the price.

4

Factory Farm Animals Are Treated Humanely

AgEdNet.com

AgEdNet.com is an agricultural information and educational service.

Most people have idealized, obsolete concepts about farm animals that need to be corrected The truth is that farmers do not treat animals as pets and farm animals have no legal rights. They are confined to crates and pens and treated as products in the modern food industry, which feeds hundreds of millions of people daily. However, farmers, ranchers, and producers treat animals humanely so that the creatures remain productive. Anti-industry advocates who believe that animals have legal rights are among the minority that would shut down the American agricultural system. The views of these extremists need to be challenged not only by producers but by those who support modern agriculture methods by choosing to eat meat, wear leather, and drink milk.

Most people today have very little knowledge of what farm animals are like, or what is required to care for them. Some urban dwellers own pets, but farm animals are not pets and cannot be treated like pets. Most of what children learn about farm animals is from children's books, movies and television, in stories that are far from realistic.

Children read about and watch farm animals act like humans. Animals in books and movies talk and reason with each

AgNetEd.com, "Understanding 'Animal Rights' Vs. 'Animal Welfare,'" agednet.com, 2004. Reproduced by permission.

other. In these stories, animals are just like people. Stories with animal characters have been a part of children's literature for generations. Children that grew up on farms could easily see the difference between real animals and storybook animals. Most of today's children do not live on a farm and have not had the experience of working with real farm animals.

Farmers, ranchers and livestock feeders strongly support the concept that animals should be raised under humane conditions.

Agriculture has been changing dramatically as farms become larger and livestock producers take advantage of new technologies and new systems for rearing and handling animals.

- It is no longer as common to see cows grazing in a quiet green pasture. Farm flocks of chickens that once gleaned waste around farmsteads have become a thing of the past. Farming is not what it once was, leaving many Americans with an idealistic image of farming. That image is generations out of date.

- An increasing number of farm animals and birds are kept in pens, crates or cages. This practice, called "confinement" rearing, saves labor and makes more efficient use of feed.

- Keeping animals confined has become a cause for public concern. Some activists maintain that keeping animals in confinement is like keeping people in jail. Others believe confinement places undue stress on animals; while producers maintain that animals are comfortable in confinement or they would not be productive.

- New questions are emerging over the altering of animals through genetic engineering. Will this practice cause increased stress on animals? Do humans have a "right" to alter animal life? Should these practices be allowed? To what extent should they be regulated?

Animal Welfare Vs. Animal Rights

The two terms above divide the full range of views on how animals should be treated. Both need to be taken into account because they represent some strongly held views. It also is important to understand clearly what these terms mean in order to take part in any discussion of animal treatment issues.

Animal welfare has to do with the proper care of animals. Farmers, ranchers and livestock feeders strongly support the concept that animals should be raised under humane conditions. Most producers do care about how their animals are treated and do not relish seeing an animal suffer.

Proper, humane treatment is also important to producers because it helps to keep animals more productive. Animals placed under undue stress will not be productive, nor will they be profitable to maintain. The concept of animal welfare means humans have more rights than animals; but humans also have the responsibility to provide humane treatment for animals.

The concept of animal rights goes far beyond protecting the physical well-being of animals. In addition, those who accept the concept of animal rights believe that animals have inherent legal and ethical rights that are the same as humans. Those who take the most extreme view on animal rights support the total elimination of all uses of animals for food, clothing, leisure or research. They favor abolishing animal agriculture entirely.

Most Americans do not agree that animals have rights similar to those of humans. A huge majority of Americans eat meat, drink milk and wear leather shoes and jackets. At the same time, most Americans strongly oppose farming practices that would allow an animal to suffer unnecessary pain or stress. That is where real issues may arise.

The Battle for Public Support

Those who want to change the way farm animals are treated often go to extremes to get attention. This often has taken the form of protest demonstrations at state fairs where livestock are being exhibited, or at the annual meetings of national livestock producer organizations. The organization People for the Ethical Treatment of Animals (PETA) has become especially well-known as the driving force behind this effort. It has been especially effective in getting national media attention to focus on suggestions that animals are being misused and should be granted more legal rights.

The objective of these protests is to gain media attention and thus sway more Americans over to an "animal rights" point of view. The two main points being made are that:

1. Animals are like people and should not be used as a source of human food or clothing.
2. Animals suffer unnecessary pain and stress due to mistreatment by farmers and producers.

Animal rights groups know that most Americans do not accept their views on animal rights. They also want to draw a large amount of media attention to their protests and hope they can raise public doubts about how well farm animals are treated. Such doubts can then result in public support to outlaw some common livestock and poultry production practices.

Some examples of specific charges activists make that will likely cause the public to be more concerned include the following:

- Pumping drugs into animals raised in confinement places undue stress on the animals and jeopardizes animal and human health.

- Using a growth-promoting hormone is cruel to animals and produces meat that is not safe for humans to eat.

- Raising animals in pens and crates is cruel treatment.

- Eating meat and eggs and drinking milk is unhealthy for humans.

- Grain fed to livestock should be used to feed starving people around the world.

Protesters are using two basic tactics in charges such as those above. One is to raise concern about the welfare of animals. The other is to create fear among consumers about meat and other animal products. Making charges such as those listed above often attracts newspaper reporters and television cameras. News coverage of their protests gives them an opportunity to repeat their charges in newspaper articles and on evening TV news shows where millions of Americans can hear and see their message.

Producer groups are often put on the defensive when these protests take place. Too often newspaper and television reporters are not well-informed about modern agricultural practices. Some reporters may be sympathetic with animal rights views.

While news reporters try to be objective, their personal points of view may sway the way questions are asked and the way facts are presented. This can make it very difficult for a producer to respond without sounding argumentative and defensive. Imagine standing in front of a TV camera and trying to answer a reporter who is asking, "If you really care about your animals, how can you kill them and eat them?"

Farm organizations and producer groups have tried to respond with their own information programs. These have taken the form of media kits for reporters as well as publications distributed to schools and events. Events such as "breakfast on the farm" programs are beneficial because they invite urban children and adults to visit farms where they can see the animals and how they are treated. Chances are, however, that such an event will not attract as many TV cameras as an animal rights protest.

When Real Issues Emerge

An issue becomes "real" when enough public concern is raised that specific public actions are proposed. So far, no one has seriously proposed a law against eating meat, or against raising livestock in confinement. But there have been calls for additional regulation.

Treatment of disabled livestock is an example. There is no way producers can prevent some animals from becoming disabled. A common cause is paralysis due to calving difficulty. News stories about mistreatment of disabled animals on farms or at slaughter plants have gained a good deal of public sympathy. Restrictive legislation has been suggested. Experts believe that the number of disabled animals passing through markets is less than 1/10 of 1 percent. While that percentage of total marketing is small, it could add up to as many as 40,000 animals per year—enough to generate significant news coverage.

Many farm organizations . . . actively support programs that encourage the humane treatment of animals.

The National Cattlemen's Beef Association has taken a proactive approach to the issue. NCBA objectives are to avoid negative news stories and to reduce public support for restrictive new legislation. To do this the NCBA developed educational material to be used at producers' meetings on the prevention and handling of disabled livestock.

Producers can win public support on animal treatment issues by following the NCBA example above. The two most important things the NCBA did and that other organizations could do are to:

1. Support and promote the humane treatment of animals among their own members. Producers must do all they can to be certain that animals are not being mistreated.

2. Keep the public and the media, as well as lawmakers, well-informed about what producers are doing to protect the welfare of animals.

Many farm organizations, such as the NCBA and the National Pork Producers' Council, actively support programs that encourage the humane treatment of animals. You will find many examples of these programs at Internet websites maintained by these groups. One example of these efforts is the labeling of meat and other livestock products as "Certified Humane Raised & Handled." This program started in early 2003 and is backed by 10 animal welfare groups. It certifies producers and processors who meet certain standards for animal treatment.

5

Large-scale Hog Operations Are Severely Polluting the Air and Water

Christopher D. Cook

Christopher D. Cook is an award-winning investigative journalist whose work has appeared in Harper's, Mother Jones, *the* Nation, *the* Economist, In These Times, *and on Alternet.com.*

Every year, factory hog farms across the United States generate billions of tons of manure creating toxic air pollution that sickens thousands of people. The manure also leaches into waterways and kills billions of fish while destroying river, estuary, bay, and wetland ecosystems. As more hogs are concentrated on fewer huge farms, this form of industrialized pork production has become the largest source of water pollution in the United States. Unless laws are enacted to stop factory animal farming, people and the environment will continue to pay a high price for the cheap bacon and pork chops at the supermarket.

Out on rural Route 4 near the crumbling farm town of Unionville, Missouri, Jeri and Lynn McKinley have an up-close view of an animal farm the likes of which George Orwell surely never imagined [in his 1945 novel]. They live next to 80,000 pigs. Crammed in Manhattan-like density, the pigs produce a suffocating methane-gas stench that "wakes you up in the middle of the night," Lynn says. Rivers of pig waste flow onto their land, polluting the water that sustains the McKinleys' cattle.

Other residents in this northern Missouri community tell of waking up nauseous on many a summer's night, blanketed by hog fumes that send them running to the bathroom to retch. Throughout the warm months, when methane concentrations settle into a thick fog, homes within miles of these animal factories reek of pig shit: curtains, carpets, and clothes are marinated in the heavy smell, which hog and cattle farmers say is far more putrid than the hog manure from traditional farming, to which they are accustomed. This is a far heavier perfume, the product of thousands of pigs stuffed in a building, their lives spent doing nothing more than standing in one place, eating, urinating, and defecating.

Rolf Christen, a cattle and grain farmer who transplanted his family from Switzerland to the north Missouri hill country in 1983, finally got sick of the nausea and realized he had to either move away or fight the offender, the agribusiness giant Premium Standard Farms (PSF). "I can't describe how terrible the odor from the lagoon, sprayfields and barns often is," Christen was quoted as saying in a 2001 report by the Clean Water Network and the Natural Resources Defense Council. "We can't keep our windows open, and sometimes you can even smell the odor through the shut windows. . . . A year or so ago, I went on vacation to a beautiful national park; when I entered my house upon my return and smelled the terrible odor, I broke down and cried."

Along with other fume-weary farmers and residents in the area, the energetic fifty-year-old Christen formed Citizens Legal Environmental Action Network, or CLEAN. In July 1997, with the hog stench no doubt in full bloom, CLEAN took PSF to court. But this was more than an odor nuisance lawsuit. They charged the hog firm with major violations of the federal Clean Water Act and Clean Air Act, alleging massive unauthorized dumping of excess hog feces onto local fields and streams. PSF, which agreed to settle the case in 2001, had already been charged with dozens of violations of state water and air laws, including numerous highly damaging spills of manure waste into streams and rivers.

Animal waste generated by concentrated feeding operations poses a real threat to the health of American waters.

The Biggest Polluters

Premium Standard Farm's pollution troubles are not isolated incidents. Agriculture, in particular today's enormous animal factory farms, "has become the biggest polluter of U.S. waterways." Those are not the excited claims of an agribusiness critic but rather a matter-of-fact statement tucked into the middle of a December 2002 *Los Angeles Times* article. Even Christine Todd Whitman, then the Environmental Protection Agency administrator, bluntly acknowledged, "Animal waste generated by concentrated feeding operations poses a real threat to the health of American waters." Whitman was safely behind the curve: potent evidence of an animal waste epidemic, emanating from mostly corporate-run concentrated animal feeding operations, or CAFOs, had been literally piling up for more than a decade.

The most concrete proof was all the dead fish—tens of millions of them killed by factory farm waste spilled into rivers and streams.

Why such carnage? Animal manure is a natural fertilizer, rich in nitrogen and phosphorus, that has been used to fortify farmland soils for centuries. But factory farms produce way too much of a good thing. In hog factories, according to a May 2000 report by the Consumers Union, pigs "are raised in closed barns, often from birth. They stand on slotted floors which allow their waste to drop below into a shallow tank which is flushed out with water." The "effluent," as the industry calls it, is then pumped into manure-filled lagoons often the size of several football fields. This type of toxic reservoir is also used by many large-scale cattle and dairy operations.

When sprayed on farmlands, as is often the case, or dumped or leaked onto the ground, concentrated levels of nitrogen and phosphorus enter water supplies and create algae blooms that choke off oxygen and kill aquatic life. Hog manure is also loaded with ammonia, which when leaked or sprayed concentrates in soil and turns into nitrate when exposed to oxygen. Nitrate, toxic to humans in low doses, is very soluble and travels quickly through groundwater, thus threatening drinking water.

The root of the pollution problem ... is easily understood: too many animals—and too much manure—concentrated on too little land.

Animal factories also generate serious air pollution. In North Carolina alone, according to an analysis by the Environmental Defense Fund, hogs send over 167 million pounds of ammonia nitrogen into the atmosphere every year—more than 458,000 pounds per day. "Blown downwind, this ammonia nitrogen subsequently rains down on sensitive rivers, estuaries, and coastal waters. . . . Studies in the North Carolina region where hog factories are clustered show that the level of ammonia in rain has doubled in the past decade."

An in-depth report published in August 2000 by a coalition of environmental groups, titled "Spills and Kills," stated, "The root of the pollution problem caused by large confined livestock facilities is easy to understand: too many animals— and too much manure—concentrated on too little land." Exacerbating this problem is the "use of woefully inadequate 'technologies' for manure management. Lax regulatory enforcement also contributes to a pollution problem that is an environmental and public health crisis in this country."

In Missouri, where PSF's hog pollution inspired citizen lawsuits, state environmental regulators repeatedly found themselves counting dead fish floating belly-up in rivers and streams near the company's swine warehouses that dot the hilltops. A single spill from one PSF lagoon in 1995 killed as many as 173,000 fish. In another case, a faulty sewage line led to the release of some 35,000 gallons of pig waste into a north-central Missouri creek. . . .

Missouri's torrent of manure is but a modest trickle when compared with North Carolina, the nation's fastest-growing hog state. Without much regulation, North Carolina's hog population ballooned between 1987 and 1997 from 2.5 million to over 10 million, even as the number of farms decreased by 75 percent. Now its swine population ranks second only to that of Iowa. The epicenter of this growth was a five-county area surrounding the world's largest hog slaughterhouse, opened in Bladen County, North Carolina, by Smithfield Foods in 1991. This one massive facility turns more than 24,000 pigs into pork each day.

As the business consolidated, the environmental crisis grew. In eastern North Carolina's Neuse River Basin alone, hog and dairy farms were producing 2.5 billion gallons of waste annually by 1995. The region also boasted 493,000 tons of chicken shit, 3.3 million pounds of dead chickens and turkeys, and 200 million pounds of nitrogen- and phosphorus-laden manure coursing through Neuse River Basin waterways, according to an investigation by the Raleigh *News and Observer*. . . .

A Tidal Wave of Manure

Hog manure exploded onto the nation's front pages in the summer of 1995, when an excrement-filled hog lagoon in North Carolina burst its seams, sending a tidal wave of 25 million gallons of nitrate-loaded manure gushing into the New River. As environmental inspectors tallied the carnage, it became clear this was the biggest, most deadly pig-waste spill yet recorded; its volume was twice the size of the Exxon Valdez oil spill. The damage was both environmental and economic: the spill killed nearly 10 million fish, and shut down 364,000 acres of coastal wetlands to shellfishing. Dead fish and poisoned rivers are bad not only for the state's $1 billion fishing business but also for tourism, North Carolina's second-leading revenue source. Tom Madison, a Republican and veteran of the Marines who founded an environmental group called the New River Foundation, commented, "You just can't get tourists to come down to North Carolina to watch dead fish float by."

In 1999, thanks to the ravages of Hurricane Floyd, North Carolina's booming hog industry was back in the news. While killing forty-eight people and racking up more than $1 billion in property destruction, the hurricane "left a vast amount of damage that might have been averted: incalculable and continuing hazards in groundwater, wells and rivers from animal waste, mostly from giant hog farms," the *New York Times* reported. "In the hurricane, feces and urine soaked the terrain and flowed into rivers from overburdened waste pits the industry calls lagoons." In a grim testimonial to the state's burgeoning corporate animal business, more than 2 million dead turkeys, chickens and hogs piled up in Floyd's aftermath, illustrated in the press by images of giant bulldozers plowing mounds of pig carcasses into something resembling mass graves.

This catastrophe was more than just an accident of nature. As the *New York Times* assessed, "Loose regulations that helped eastern North Carolina become the nation's biggest producer of turkeys and the second-biggest of hogs have come back to haunt the state's public health and its environment." According to a Sierra Club report titled "Corporate Hogs at the Public Trough," state lawmakers, fattened by hog-industry campaign contributions, doled out generous tax breaks and subsidies to large factory-farm outfits owned by politically connected businessmen.

Most prominent among these is a hog magnate named Wendell Murphy, the owner of Murphy Family Farms and previously a powerful state legislator who chaired the North Carolina Senate's agriculture committee. One of his legislative accomplishments, known as Murphy's Law, exempted factory farms from local zoning laws that might hinder the size of confinement houses and lagoons, especially along delicate floodplains. Journalist David Case wrote, "For a mere million or so dollars [in campaign donations], the hog barons were able to treat the eastern part of the state as one big sewer." In 1997 the state prohibited building any new hog lagoons within a floodplain; but many of these "porcine ecological time bombs," as Case described them, remain in these precarious estuary-like hot spots.

People living within two miles of the hog operation suffered far more headaches, nasal and throat irritations, heartburn, vomiting, diarrhea, burning eyes, and skin rashes.

A National Epidemic

Lest the biggest factory farm spills appear as isolated disasters involving a few bad players, take a look at the situation nationwide. Fish kills caused by factory farm discharges have become epidemic: in ten states, more than 1,000 documented manure spills wiped out an astounding total of 13 million fish between 1995 and 1998. But even that figure pales when compared with estimates by the EPA that *Pfiesteria piscicida,* an organism in manure, has killed more than 2 billion fish in rivers, estuaries and coastal areas in the Chesapeake Bay region of North Carolina, Maryland, and Virginia.

The total volume of factory-farm waste is simply staggering. There is enough manure waste produced on these factory farms each year to fill 52 million large eighteen-wheeler semi trucks. This convoy of excrement would stretch bumper-to-bumper all the way across the United States—148 times.

In 1997, the United States Senate Agriculture Committee investigated the waste crisis and came to the following conclusion: including cattle, hogs, chickens, and turkeys, the nation's animal industries produce an astounding total of 1.3 billion tons of manure waste each year. That's five tons for every U.S. citizen—130 times the amount of human waste produced per year in America.

The Senate Agriculture Committee's tally:

- The [California] Central Valley's 1,600 dairies generate more waste than a city of 21 million people.

- Some 600 million chickens raised on the ecologically fragile Delmarva Peninsula (in eastern Delaware, Maryland, and Virginia) produce over 3.2 billion pounds of raw waste a year, which contains as much nitrogen as the waste from a city of 500,000.

- A 50,000-acre swine operation in southwest Utah "designed to produce 2.5 million hogs annually" will generate "a potential waste output greater than the entire city of Los Angeles." (The facility currently churns out 1 million hogs a year.)The Senate report concluded, "As animals become increasingly concentrated in certain regions of the country and on larger operations, there is not always enough cropland to use all of the manure as fertilizer. These increasing concentrations of manure mean that the risk of water pollution from waste spills, runoff from fields and leakage from storage facilities is also increasing." . . .

There Goes the Neighborhood

Living next door to thousands of hogs may indeed be bad for your health. In one of the few systematic surveys to examine the public health impacts of large-scale hog operations, Steve Wing, an epidemiologist with the University of North Carolina, found that daily whiffs of hog-factory waste appear to cause sinus problems, excessive coughing, headaches, nausea, and diarrhea.

Wing and his research team interviewed three communities—one near a hog-raising factory, another near a cattle facility, and a control group far away from any animal yards—about a wide range of health symptoms. People living within two miles of the hog operation suffered far more headaches, nasal and throat irritations, heartburn, vomiting, diarrhea, burning eyes, and skin rashes than the other two groups.

A similar 1997 study on the health effects of a hog operation in Iowa also documented high rates of upper-respiratory and mucous-membrane problems among residents living near giant pig factory farms. "The constellation of symptoms they reported are almost identical to the kinds of symptoms that we find among workers inside the facilities," says Kendall Thu, assistant professor of anthropology at Northern Illinois University, who helped conduct the study. Epidemiologists have also documented serious health problems, such as chronic bronchitis and occupational asthma, among workers in hog confinement facilities; more than 25 percent report suffering at least one chronic respiratory ailment.

According to Gary Grant, director of Concerned Citizens of Tillery, a grassroots community group in eastern North Carolina, most hog factories in the Tar Heel State "are locating in rural communities that we call the avenues of least resistance—primarily African American, aged, and poor communities." Research prepared by his group uses census data to show that North Carolina's top hog-producing counties have high African American populations and poverty rates. Thirteen of the top fifteen counties are at least 25 percent African American, and about 30 percent of their residents are at or below the poverty line.

Immediately after Wing released his findings, representatives of North Carolina's booming $1.8 billion pork industry pressured him and his assistant, Susanne Wolf, to identify the community where he had done his research. The North Carolina Pork Council hired a powerhouse law firm to secure the researchers' records, including documents that could be used to identify study participants who had been guaranteed confidentiality.

"We released our study at ten a.m. and by five p.m. we had a letter from the industry's attorney," Wing said in an interview. In the letter, an industry attorney, Charles Case, raised the possibility of a defamation lawsuit. Ultimately this threat brought the hog industry some bad press and the suit was dropped. Case insisted the industry merely wanted "to see if the results are reproducible" and did not seek "any information that discloses . . . the identity of the people they interviewed."

Wing said the hog industry's aggressive reaction was "unprecedented." He was informed he could be arrested if he failed to turn over correspondence, community maps, and other data that would reveal the community he studied. He asserted that the documents demanded by the industry were "not restricted to things that would be considered necessary in academia to replicate the study." Wing turned over most of the documents, but resisted the industry's "harassing" demands for detailed community maps and demographic data that would reveal what town he studied.

Apart from his interest in protecting academic freedom, Wing expressed concern about the hog industry's threatening tactics. "I have spent many years building trust and relationships with people in eastern North Carolina," he explained. "I'm obligated to protect them from having their identity revealed to an organization that has a history of intimidating people. If they want to know personal information about these communities, forget it."

Such fears may be warranted. In June 1998, attorneys for a North Carolina hog farmer threatened to sue Elsie Herring, a black woman in her nineties who had complained repeatedly to state water-quality officials about the farmer's alleged over-spraying of hog manure near her home in the town of Wallace. In a letter to Herring, the farmer's attorney promised to sue her for compensatory and punitive damages and impose a restraining order if she continued filing "false and groundless" complaints. "If you violate any such restraining order," the lawyer warned, "we will ask the court to put you in prison for contempt."

6

Large Hog Farms Do Not Significantly Impact Water Quality

Dennis T. Avery and Alex Avery

Dennis T. Avery and Alex Avery are directors of the Hudson Institute's Center for Global Food Issues in Washington, D.C.

Animal rights activists, environmentalists, and journalists have linked large animal farms to water pollution in many states including North Carolina, home to the nation's second-largest concentration of hog farms. Anti-farm activists have charged that the nutrients in pig manure have created mass algae blooms in rivers that have choked off oxygen to aquatic creatures—a process known as eutrophication. Despite the dire claims of environmentalists, studies have shown that rivers in North Carolina have not been contaminated from hog farms even as the number of pigs in the state has increased tenfold since 1997. These facts have been ignored by reporters who have printed negative stories about hog farms. The public needs to be made aware that the negative views of environmentalists are simply wrong and that hog farmers provide low-cost, high-quality food to consumers.

Although there have always been hog farmers in North Carolina, the industry was fairly small until the mid-1980s. At that time, a major new hog slaughter plant opened in the state, and dozens of new confinement hog farms were set up to take advantage of eastern North Carolina's low employment levels. As a result, hog farming in eastern North Carolina took off in the late 1980s and early '90s.

Dennis T. Avery and Alex Avery, "Hog Farms No Threat to North Carolina Water Quality," *Environment and Climate News*, March 1, 2004. Reproduced by permission.

The core of this hog farm expansion was located in Sampson and Duplin counties, two adjoining counties drained by two rivers—the Black and the Northeast Cape Fear. Between 1985 and 1995, the hog population in these two coastal watersheds increased tenfold, from 500,000 to 5.5 million animals. By 1997, this area accounted for 10 percent of the total U.S. swine inventory. (The balance of the state's hog population, consisting of some two million animals, is scattered throughout the coastal plain.)

The rapid expansion of the hog population, the growing number of larger, integrated farms, and the central role of corporations alarmed environmentalists and social activists, who generally do not like either large corporations or large, intensive farming operations.

The controversy began in February 1995, when the *Raleigh News & Observer* ran a harsh, five-article series titled, "Boss Hog: North Carolina's Pork Revolution." The series detailed the explosive growth of the industry and questioned the environmental and social impacts of intensive hog production.

The top concern cited in the articles was the "9.5 million tons" of hog waste coming from the "megalopolis of seven million animals that live in metal confinement barns" in eastern North Carolina. The articles charged hog waste was polluting both groundwater and the state's rivers and streams, harming the environment and posing a potential health threat to nearby residents. The "Boss Hog" series netted the *News & Observer* the 1996 Pulitzer Prize for Public Service Journalism.

No Harm to Water Quality

Yet there is still no evidence whatsoever that water quality has gotten worse in North Carolina. As researchers at Duke University's Nicholas School of the Environment noted in research published in 2000:

> [The enrichment of the river with nutrients from manure or] eutrophication [of the Neuse River estuary] is believed

to have worsened in recent years. . . . However, our results indicate that while nitrogen concentrations have not changed significantly, *they may have declined slightly overall in the lower river and estuary in the last 22 years.* Additionally, phosphorus concentrations have dropped considerably at all locations since the mid 1980s. . . .

The Duke researchers speculated it was the *improved* water quality—the lower levels of phosphorus—that changed the critical ratio of nitrogen-to-phosphorus, leading to an increase in algal blooms in the Neuse estuary. This created the false impression that the water quality was declining. All too predictably, not a single North Carolina newspaper reported on this research or its implications in the debate over the environmental effects of hog farming.

There is, in fact, strong evidence that hog farms haven't harmed water quality in the region. In early 2003, at the request of the Cape Fear River Assembly, the authors of this article set out to perform an extensive review of the historical water quality data in the Black and Northeast Cape Fear rivers (home to roughly 80 percent of the state's hogs) for the period before and after the hog farm expansion.

When we called the Water Quality Division at the North Carolina Department of Environment and Natural Resources (DENR) to obtain the data, the director declined to release it to us. He claimed an analysis of that data already had been conducted as part of the DENR's five-year environmental assessment published in 1999.

But the DENR's report omitted water quality data for the Black and Northeast Cape Fear rivers completely. Instead, the report focused on "biological indicators" of aquatic health (such as inventories of fish) that implied a slight worsening of river conditions since the previous environmental assessment in 1994.

After major flooding and hurricanes in 1995–96, North Carolina received federal grants to clear fallen trees and woody debris clogging rivers and streams, to prevent future flooding. The DENR report admitted this factor made it impossible to blame hog farms for the decreases in biological indicators in the regional waters:

"Zealous pursuit of this goal often totally cleared all woody material from the stream, *material that is a critical habitat for both fish and invertebrates.* For some streams, heavy machinery was used along the banks. . . . It is difficult to separate out the effects of de-snagging in these streams from the potential impact of increased numbers of hog farms within the same area."

The data clearly show the water quality within and downstream of the hog farming areas is as good now as it was before the hog industry expansion.

Data Exonerate Hog Farms

The 1999 DENR report included water quality data for other rivers within the Cape Fear basin . . . so why did the agency omit only the data for the two rivers draining the intensive hog farming areas? Why did the DENR instead rely on a flawed proxy of water quality? When we insisted on examining the data ourselves, the head of the Division of Water Quality at DENR refused to provide it. It wasn't until legal action was threatened that we were provided the data.

The data clearly show the water quality within and downstream of the hog farming areas is as good now as it was before the hog industry expansion. Despite a tenfold increase in the hog populations, there has been no increase in nutrient concentrations, no reduction in dissolved oxygen levels, and no increase in sediment loads.

Incredibly, during nearly a decade of intense, acrimonious debate between environmental activists and hog farmers— whipped into a frenzy by articles like the *News & Observer* 's "Boss Hog" series—the DENR suppressed its own water quality data and failed to inform the public and policymakers of the real conditions of the rivers and streams in question.

In this way, the government of North Carolina effectively stole the great economic opportunity of hog farm expansion from some of its poorest citizens.

Bad News Sells

Our own report was not totally ignored by the media. The *Wilmington Star-News* ran a single article on the study, published before our report was even written. The headline to the story tells you everything you need to know about press coverage of the controversy: "Defense of Hog Farms Full of Holes, Scientist Says."

The public is too often given only one-sided, simplistic, pessimistic versions of environmental realities by the news media, and even by government agencies and researchers.

Journalism has never been more important to our society . . . and, perhaps, never less adequate.

7

Large-scale Confinement Operations Are Not Necessary

John Ikerd

John Ikerd is professor emeritus of agricultural economics at the University of Missouri in Columbia.

The number of factory animal farms, known as confinement animal feeding operations (CAFOs), is growing at an explosive rate. These huge operations produce millions of pigs, chickens, and cows for American supermarkets. Proponents of CAFOs, such as government agencies, large corporations, and equipment manufacturers, promote many alleged benefits of CAFOs. However, contrary to the assertions of agribusiness advocates, CAFOs are not more efficient, do not produce cheaper food, do not provide benefits to surrounding communities, and are not necessary to feed starving people in developing nations. Family farmers and consumers need to closely examine the claims made by CAFO promoters and realize that the profit motive, not concern for the well-being of others, is driving the move to megafarms in the United States.

Most people in the *agricultural establishment* seem to accept large-scale confinement animal feeding operations (CAFOs) as an economic necessity. They see the trend away from smaller diversified family farms and toward larger specialized, confinement operations as being driven by impersonal market forces, tending toward ever-greater economic ef-

John Ikerd, "Do We Need Large-Scale Confinement Animal Feeding Operations?" Speech for the Food and Society Networking Conference, panel on Revitalizing Non-confinement Raised Meats, sponsored by the W.K. Kellogg Foundation, Olympic Valley, California, April 20–22, 2004. Reproduced by permission of the author.

ficiency. They point out, often without any supporting evidence, that CAFOs are more economically efficient than are smaller non-confinement operations. They claim the trend toward CAFOs is a logical market response to consumer preferences—that consumers demand, or at least prefer, the uniformity of quality achievable only with standardized production systems.

Livestock farmers are told that they must adopt the new industrial technologies that make CAFOs feasible, if they expect to have a future in farming. Current changes in the meat animal industry are inevitable, they are told, because they are driven by the irresistible forces of a free market economy, and thus, cannot and should not be controlled. Leaders in agricultural communities are told they must accept, if not embrace, this new kind of industrial agriculture, or their communities will be left behind. CAFOs are needed to support local jobs, local tax dollars, and related local economic development. Rural residents who oppose CAFOs are labeled as naïve, idealistic, uninformed obstructionists to economic progress.

The public, in general, is told that even more CAFOs will be necessary to feed the hungry people of a rapidly growing global society. For this reason, the *agricultural establishment* proclaims, we must continue to expand our productive capacity, even during times when markets are depressed by surplus production. While the wealthy of the future may continue to be well fed, we must have abundant supplies of cheap food, including cheap meat, if the poor are to be spared from hunger and malnutrition. CAFOs are needed for humanitarian reasons, so we are told.

But, what is the validity of these claims.

- Do farmers need large-scale confinement animal feeding operations to achieve efficient, low-cost production?

- Do we need an industrial, standardized meat production system to satisfy consumer preferences?

- Do farmers and rural communities need these large-scale, corporate contract operations to provide employment and economic development opportunities?

- Do we need an industrial approach to agriculture to feed the poor and hungry of the world?

The answer to each of these questions is, NO!

All popular myths are supported by elements of truth. But, the elements of truth in these cases are not sufficient to validate the truth of the popular claims regarding CAFOs. *No one really needs CAFOs.*

Smaller "well managed" hog operations are more efficient and have lower production costs than do "average" mega-sized hog operations.

Do we need CAFOs for efficient, low cost production?

No! The claim that large-scale confinement operations are more efficient is a myth - widely promoted, but still a myth. The element of truth in this case is that large-scale, CAFO operations, in general, are more efficient than are many smaller, non-confinement operations. The reality, however, is that many, if not most, smaller, non-confinement operations are more efficient than are the larger confinement operations. Also, many smaller hog operations are not nearly as efficient or as profitable as they could be.

For the sake of brevity, the specific comparisons provided here are limited mostly to hog and pork production. However, similar relationships exist for comparisons of large-scale, confinement beef, dairy, and poultry operations with smaller, non-confinement systems. In the case of beef and dairy production, the most popular non-confinement alternative is grass-based operations. In the case of poultry, the more promising alternatives are pastured and free-range chicken, turkey, and egg production. For hogs, two popular alternatives have emerged. One alternative includes a wide range of "pasture-based" systems, most of which include some type of housing for some part of the production period, but allow hogs free access to pasture most of the time. The other alternative involves "hoop house" production, including both farrowing and feeding operations, where hogs are produced in deeply bedded greenhouse-like structures.

Confinement, pasture, and hoop house operations may vary widely in size. However, a typical pasture or hoop house production unit might involve 50–100 sows or 1,000–2,000 market hogs, whereas a typical large-scale confinement unit might involve 600–1000 sows or 12,000–20,000 market hogs. Both pasture-based and hoop house hog production systems avoid many of the animal health, human health, animal welfare, and waste disposal problems associated with large-scale confinement animal feeding operations. Most of these problems quite simply are unavoidable when too many animals and too much waste are confined in too little space.

Returning to the question of productivity and economic efficiency, state universities that have maintained swine record systems over the years have shown consistently that smaller "well managed" hog operations are more efficient and have lower production costs than do "average" mega-sized hog operations. Typically, the most-efficient one-third, sometimes up to one-half, of smaller operations is shown to be more efficient than are "average" mega hog operations. . . .

Individual management ability has a far greater impact on efficiency and profitability than does the type of system.

The element of truth supporting the efficiency myth is that mega operations tend to be more "consistently efficient." Thus, mega operations, in general, may be more efficient than the "least efficient" one-third, or possibly one-half, of all smaller operations. Thus, larger operations are able to survive and make profits at price levels that will drive these "less-efficient," smaller producers out of business. Consistency in efficiency has allowed larger CAFO operations to get a strong foothold in the hog-pork industry, even without having any inherent advantage in overall economic efficiency.

The one-third to one-half of smaller operations that are already more efficient than CAFOs have opportunities to become even more efficient in the future, through more-effective management of their unique types of operations. A major obstacle for smaller producers today is the lack of encouragement and support from the *agricultural establishment*. . . . [M]any of the technologies that typically give large operations an economic advantage are adaptable to smaller operations, but are simply less frequently used by smaller operations. In addition, very little research and extension work has been devoted in recent years to improving the efficiency of non-confinement livestock operations. . . .

The bottom line . . . is the economic efficiency is not significantly different among confinement, hoop house, or pasture based systems of hog production. Individual management ability has a far greater impact on efficiency and profitability than does the type of system. These facts are rarely contested among those who are familiar with cost of production data for the various types of hog production systems. There simply is no compelling economic efficiency advantage for large-scale CAFO operations.

So why do some farmers choose CAFOs instead of hoop house or pasture systems? Primarily because CAFOs are easier to manage, and thus, each producer can manage more hogs. If a confinement producer can produce and sell more hogs, he or she can make more profits in total, even if profit per hog sold is no more, or even less, than profits for hogs produced in non-confinement systems. . . .

Do We Need CAFOs to Satisfy Consumer Preferences?

No! The claim that the trend toward large-scale confinement animal feeding operations is being driven by consumer demand is another industry-promoted myth. The element of truth in this myth is that consumers do prefer, if not demand, "consistency" in their products. We want the pork chop we buy this week to taste the same as the one we bought last week, if we buy the same kind of chop in the same store, and if it looks the same as the one we bought last week. Consistency is necessary if we are to be able to choose the things that will provide us with satisfaction and avoid the things that will not. But, this natural preference for consistency does not mean, or even suggest, that we all want the same thing. Consistency and variety are two distinct concepts. We don't all prefer pork chops that look and taste the same.

The incentive for consistency and control is to enhance corporate profits—not to satisfy consumer preferences.

In fact, a basic premise of economics is that consumers have different tastes and preferences. In basic economic theory, the utility of usefulness of anything is determined by form, place, time, and possession or individuality. To know what anything is worth, we must first know what it is (form), where it is (place), when it is available (time), and finally, who has it and who wants it (individuality). The same thing at the same place at the same time may have a different value to any two individuals. We don't all prefer or value the same things. To respond effectively to consumer preferences, we must give different people the different things that they individually prefer, not give them all the same thing.

Economies of scale in industrial production arise from specialization and standardization of production processes. Once production has been specialized and standardized, it can be routinized and mechanized, so that it can be carried out at lower costs, in large-scale operations. Large-scale food processors, distributors, and retailers gain their economic advantage in the market place by specializing in the performance of standardized functions. They achieve greater economic efficiency in processing (changing form), distribution (changing place), and packaging/storage (changing time), only if they can convince large numbers of consumers to accept the same specialized, standardized products (to ignore their individuality).

The demand for uniformity in pork production, for "standardization," today is coming from food processors and distributors, not from food consumers. Pork processors and distributors, not consumers, benefit from a system characterized by consistency in breeds, feeds, medications, growing environment, and market weights. To achieve this consistency, they must have control of the system. The desire for consistency and control by processors and distributions, not consumer preference, is the driving force behind the trend toward large-scale CAFO production—specifically toward corporately controlled, "contract" production. . . .

Communities who welcome CAFOs to their area will only exacerbate the problems of decline in family farms and rural economic decay.

Processors and distributors of pork, beef, and milk are attempting to follow the vertical integration model developed in the poultry industry. Once a few large poultry integrators had gained control of the industry - through comprehensive production contracts with growers, utilizing large-scale poultry CAFOs—they were able to stabilize poultry supplies and prices at levels that essentially ensured the long run profitability of their operations. The incentive for consistency and control is to enhance corporate profits—not to satisfy consumer preferences. Once markets lose their economic competitiveness, i.e., are no longer characterized by a large number of small firms, the consumer is no longer "king."

Do We Need CAFOs for Farmers and Rural Communities?

No! The myth that CAFOs will provide desirable employment opportunities is most used to promote agricultural industrialization among farmers and rural community leaders. The element of truth supporting this myth is that the economic viability of traditional mid-sized family farms is in question, as is the future of many rural communities. Over the past few decades, numbers of small, part-time farming operations have increased modestly and large-scale, contract operations have increased dramatically, but the "farmers in the middle" are disappearing. Fewer farm families mean fewer people to shop on "Main Street," to attend local schools and churches, and to participate in local public affairs. In addition, the smaller farming operations, although larger in number, produce a small proportion of total agriculture products using a small proportion of agricultural inputs. The large agribusiness operations often by-pass rural communities, both in purchasing inputs and marketing their products. Thus, rural communities suffer economically and socially as the "farmers in the middle" disappear.

The fallacy in this argument is that communities who welcome CAFOs to their area will only exacerbate the problems of decline in family farms and rural economic decay. For example, the number of hog farms in the U.S. dropped from almost 700,000 to less than 100,000 between 1980 and 2002, the period during which CAFOs largely replaced diversified family hog farms. Obviously, the trend toward more CAFO operations has been a primary cause of this decline in family hog farms. How can still more CAFOs be considered as a logical solution to the problem? Certainly, a larger proportion of the surviving hog farmers have large corporate-contract, CAFO operations, but this is true only because a larger number of smaller family-sized hog operations have been driven out of business by CAFOs.

Virtually all of the economic benefits go to corporate investors and managers who live nowhere near communities where their contract operations are located.

Some farmers and some communities may view the survival question from a purely selfish perspective. Even if more large CAFO operations mean fewer family farms and fewer viable rural communities, at least "their" farm or "their" community will survive. If one farmer doesn't build a CAFO, another one will. If one community doesn't welcome CAFOs, another one will. The farmers who refuse the CAFO option and the communities that discourage CAFOs in their area simply may not survive. Again, there are elements of truth in these arguments, but also fundamental fallacies.

The fact of the matter is that CAFOs are an integral part of a corporately controlled food chain, in which producers have no power to bargain for a profit or even for an equitable return on their investment. Even in cases where producer-owned CAFOs are not yet under corporate contract, they soon will be. As is the case for poultry, and increasingly for hogs, CAFO producers who are not under contract will find they have no markets. And once under contract, they have no bargaining power to negotiate for fair and equitable treatment. In addition, contract producers make none of the important production and marketing decisions, take very little production or market risk, and thus, have little opportunity to realize profits. They are hog house landlords and contract "janitors," but certainly are not farmers, in any traditional sense of the occupation.

As rural communities that welcome CAFOs soon discover, the promised positive effects on the local economy never materialize. Virtually all of the economic benefits go to corporate investors and managers who live nowhere near communities where their contract operations are located. In many cases, communities have granted tax incentives to outside investors, which have erased any potential benefits from increased property taxes. In others, the increased demands on local public services, including road and bridge repairs, have added far more to local government costs than corporate agriculture has added to local tax revenues. The new jobs created by CAFOs are far fewer than the family farmers they displace. Most children from these communities still leave for better opportunities elsewhere. And, those who remain behind are left with the dissention among neighbors and the ecological mess that invariably accompanies CAFOs as they enter a community. Farmers and rural communities don't need CAFOs.

If a country has a surplus of employable people who need to be productively employed, CAFOs will simply make employment problems worse.

Do We Need CAFOs to Feed the Poor and Hungry of the World?

No! It's difficult to find an element of truth in this popular myth. If one exists, it's probably that it takes fewer people to produce more meat, milk, or eggs in CAFOs than in non-confinement animal operations. In the case of hogs, various studies have shown that CAFOs may require only 33 to 85 percent as many workers as non-confinement operations to produce a given number of hogs—depending on the nature of the comparisons. If a country has a scarcity of people capable of producing hogs, CAFOs may provide a significant advantage in producing pork. However, if a country has a surplus of employable people who need to be productively employed, CAFOs will simply make employment problems worse.

Nothing to date indicates that CAFOs increase a country's production capacity. For example, trends in U.S. hog production over the past fifty years show no significant increase in pork production. During this period, hog production in the U.S. shifted dramatically from nearly all hogs produced on small, diversified family farming operations to a large percentage of all hogs produced in large-scale CAFOs. . . . The trends in consumption of pork and other meats over the past fifty years simply parallel trends in population and in shifting consumer tastes and preferences rather than trends in production capacity. Nothing indicates that the U.S. could not produce much more pork and other meats than are being produced today without relying on a single CAFO operation.

Global population may well double again by the middle of the current century. But, nothing indicates that the U.S., or others country of the world, will be better able to produce enough meat to feed the poor and hungry people of the world with CAFOs than with non-confinement animal operations. In fact, there is reason to believe the trend toward large-scale, corporately controlled CAFO will result in more, rather than fewer, hungry people in the future.

The real issue in feeding the world's hungry is not total production capacity, but instead, the unequal distribution of income and wealth between the hungry and the well fed. The corporate industrialization of animal agriculture will put control of meat production in the hands of a few giant multinational corporations, which will be motivated solely by the necessity for profits and growth to satisfy their stockholders. Those who can afford to pay the price of meat necessary to generate those profits will eat and those who cannot afford the price will not. In addition, turning potential family hog farmers into corporate "serfs," through oppressive contractual arrangements, will simply serve to widen the gap between the haves and have-nots—leaving even more people without money, without meat, and without food. A far more logical approach to feeding the hungry is to enable more people in more places, all around the world, to produce their own hogs and pork, on a modest scale, in their own countries and communities. That way, more people can both eat well and earn additional income to meet other needs.

It may take larger numbers of more thoughtful hog farmers, in the U.S. and around the world, to produce enough hogs to feed more people better with non-confinement operations than it would take to produce the same number of hogs in CAFOs. But, it's far more likely that the hogs will be produced and that the poor will be well fed if hogs are produced in smaller, geographically dispersed non-confinement operations. And, what's wrong with providing more employment opportunities for more people—in hog farming or in any other respectable occupation? Nothing indicates that we need large-scale, corporate CAFOs to feed the poor and hungry of the world.

8

Large Meat Processing Plants Are Hazardous to Workers

Human Rights Watch

Human Rights Watch is the largest human rights organization based in the United States. The organization conducts fact-finding investigations into human rights abuses in all regions of the world and publishes those findings in dozens of books and reports every year.

Slaughtering animals in huge industrial meatpacking plants is one of the most hazardous jobs in America. Employees in these meat factories work long hours with sharp knives, toxic chemicals, and dangerous machinery. As a result, many meat packers experience debilitating wounds, crippled hands, amputations, crushed limbs, and even violent deaths. Those who complain about treacherous working conditions risk losing their jobs which only pay about $10 an hour. Owners of large industrialized slaughterhouses are violating the human rights of their workers, a problem government regulators must address as soon as possible.

Working in the meatpacking or poultry processing industry is notoriously dangerous. Almost every worker interviewed by Human Rights Watch for this report began with the story of a serious injury he or she suffered in a meat or poultry plant, injuries reflected in their scars, swellings, rashes, amputations, blindness, or other afflictions. At least they survived.

Human Rights Watch, "Worker Health and Safety in the Meat and Poultry Industry: Meat and Poultry Industry Dangers," January 2005. © 2005 Human Rights Watch. Reproduced by permission.

On October 9, 2003, thirty-one-year-old Jason Kelly was repairing leaks in "hydrolizer" equipment used to process chicken feathers to make a pet-food additive at Tyson Foods' River Valley animal feed plant in Texarkana, Texas. The hydrolizer was leaking hydrogen sulfide, a poisonous gas created by decaying organic matter. According to an OSHA [Occupational Health and Safety Administration] investigator's report, Tyson did not give Kelly respiratory gear to guard against inhalation of the poison, failed to label hazardous chemicals, and failed to train workers how to detect those chemicals in case of a leak.

Kelly died of asphyxiation, according to a coroner's report, due to "acute hydrogen sulfide intoxication." Tyson is contesting an OSHA citation and fine in connection with Kelly's death, arguing that the cause of death has not been conclusively determined.

Five weeks after Kelly's death, on the morning of November 20, 2003, twenty-five-year-old Glen Birdsong was working alone cleaning a holding tank near the loading dock at the Smithfield Foods hog processing plant in Tar Heel, North Carolina. The tank held mucosa mixed with sodium bisulfite intended for use as a clotting medicine ingredient. The hose Birdsong was using got caught in the tank. Birdsong climbed down a ladder to free the hose. Coworkers later found him at the bottom of the ladder unconscious and not breathing. Attempts to resuscitate him failed. He died overcome by fumes inside the tank. "They didn't tell him about the dangers, and they didn't give him a safety belt to get pulled out of there in case he fell in," coworkers told Human Rights Watch.

On March 10, 2004, the North Carolina Division of Occupational Safety and Health, which is authorized under OSHA "state plan" provisions to administer the federal safety law, cited Smithfield for a "serious" violation, namely: "the employer did not inform exposed employees, by posting danger signs or by any other equally effective means, that the tanker was a permit-required confined space and of the danger imposed." On April 19, the state agency fined the company $4,323 for the violation. The fine was reduced after applying a 25 percent discount for the company's "basic" health and safety program and a 10 percent discount for "minimal employer disruption" of the state's inspection of the site of Birdsong's death.

Anecdotal evidence of the dangers in meat and poultry plants is backed up by hard numbers. The industry has the highest rate of injury and illness in the manufacturing sector. As one Nebraska expert explains:

> Despite the hardhats, goggles, earplugs, stainless-steel mesh gloves, plastic forearm guards, chain-mail aprons and chaps, leather weightlifting belts, even baseball catcher's shin guards and hockey masks . . . the reported injury and illness rate for meatpacking was a staggering 20 per hundred full-time workers in 2001. This is two-and-a-half times greater than the average manufacturing rate . . . and almost four times more than the overall rate for private industry. . . .

Nearly one hundred night shift cleaning workers in the [North Carolina] meatpacking industry suffered amputations and crushings of body parts in the period [from] 1999–2003.

A special investigative report in 2003 by the *Omaha World-Herald* documented death, lost limbs, and other serious injuries in Nebraska meatpacking industry plants since 1999. Much of the evidence involved night shift cleaners, most of them undocumented workers. OSHA documents dryly recorded what happened:

- "Cleaner killed when hog-splitting saw is activated."

- "Cleaner dies when he is pulled into a conveyer and crushed."

- "Cleaner loses legs when a worker activates the grinder in which he is standing."

- "Cleaner loses hand when he reaches under a boning table to hose meat from chain."

- "Hand crushed in rollers when worker tries to catch a scrubbing pad that he dropped."

In all, the report concluded, nearly one hundred night shift cleaning workers in the state meatpacking industry suffered amputations and crushings of body parts in the period (1999–2003) reviewed by the investigative team. These severe injuries are just the tip of an iceberg of thousands of lacerations, contusions, burns, fractures, punctures and other forms of what the medical profession calls traumatic injuries, distinct from the endemic phenomenon in the industry of repetitive stress or musculoskeletal injury.

The employer's focus on the bottom line all too often sacrifices worker safety and health.

Eric Schlosser documented a similarly gruesome string of deaths in the mid-1990s:

> At the Monfort plant in Grand Island, Nebraska, Richard Skala was beheaded by a dehiding machine. Carlos Vincente ... was pulled into the cogs of a conveyer belt at an Excel plant in Fort Morgan, Colorado, and torn apart. Lorenzo Marin, Sr. fell from the top of a skinning machine ... struck his head on the concrete floor of an IBP plant in Columbus Junction, Iowa, and died.... Salvador Hernandez-Gonzalez had his head crushed by a pork-loin processing machine at an IBP plant in Madison, Nebraska. At a National Beef plant in Liberal, Kansas, Homer Stull climbed into a blood collection tank to clean it, a filthy tank thirty feet high. Stull was overcome by hydrogen sulfide fumes. Two coworkers climbed into the tank and tried to rescue him. All three men died.

Part of the Operating System

Slaughtering and carving up animals is inherently dangerous work, but the dangers are accentuated by company operational choices. Profit margins per chicken or per cut of meat are very low, often a few pennies a pound, so competitive advantage rests on squeezing out the highest volume of production in the shortest possible time.

Greater margins exist further along the production and marketing chain where value is added in specialty foods and prepared foods. However, in the basic slaughtering and early-stage processing plants, the employer's focus on the bottom line all too often sacrifices worker safety and health. As one industry expert says, "The impact of narrow [profit] margins on working conditions for hourly employees at meat and poultry plants is palpable. In the meat and poultry industry, the search for faster and better ways to slaughter and process meat and livestock is relentless."

Putting workers at greater risk is sometimes a conscious calculation. In a revealing exchange in a 2003 trial involving an alleged scheme by Tyson Foods to smuggle undocumented immigrant workers into its plants, a Tyson manager described the company's decision to eliminate a "mid-shift wash down" by dropping room temperature from the high sixties to fifty degrees.

The wash down was a brief, intensive cleaning operation that allowed workers a short rest while microbe buildup in work areas was eliminated. In the new system, the room was chilled to reduce microbes. The manager testified that Tyson eliminated the wash down and the workers' brief respite so that "more production can be achieved." He said that upper management rejected his recommendation for freezer suits, better gloves, and other more protective equipment for workers in the new, colder environment.

The impact on the workers was predictable. As the manager testified:

It's so hard on them, they were complaining of bursitis, arthritis, and increased musculoskeletal problems. And, also, we depended upon our current workers, naturally, to refer us incoming workers, and that stopped because nobody was—people weren't going home and saying Tyson is a good place to work, they were going home saying we're freezing.

Meatpackers try to maximize the volume of animals that go through the plant by increasing the speed at which animals are processed.

Why Is It So Dangerous?

Key features of meat and poultry industry labor make it rife with hazards to life, limb, and health. Here are the chief dangers:

Meatpackers try to maximize the volume of animals that go through the plant by increasing the speed at which animals are processed. The speed of the processing line is thus directly related to profits. However, the fact that line speed is also directly related to injuries has not prompted federal or state regulators to set line speed standards based on health and safety considerations.

The sheer volume and speed of slaughtering operations in the meat and poultry industry create enormous danger. Workers labor amid high-speed automated machinery moving chickens and carcasses past them at a hard to imagine velocity: four hundred head of beef per hour, one thousand hogs per hour, thousands of broilers per hour, all the time workers pulling and cutting with sharp hooks, knives, and other implements.

Meat and poultry workers interviewed by Human Rights Watch and by other researchers consistently cite the speed of the lines as the main source of danger. "The chain goes so fast that it doesn't give the animals enough time to die," said one beef plant worker. Another told of life under her foreman on the line: "'Speed, Ruth, work for speed!' he shouted as he stood over me. 'One cut! One cut! One cut for the skin; one cut for the meat. Get those pieces through!'"

Another beef slaughterhouse worker described what went on in his plant: "When I started working, there were fifteen chuck boners on each line . . . 380 chain speed [cattle per hour] was considered fast; you had to have sixteen or seventeen chuck boners for that. . . . [later] they were doing 400 an hour, with thirteen or fourteen chuck boners."

A 2002 investigative report in the *Denver Post* described the experience of workers at a Swift & Co. meatpacking plant in Greeley, Colorado who "can barely move" at the end of their shift, "exhausted from working on a line that turns live animals into processed meat as fast as six times a minute."

Workers told the reporter that "supervisors apply constant pressure to keep the line moving" and described:

> [A] world in which they are driven, sometimes insulted and humiliated, to keep the plant's production up. "From the time you enter, you're told that if the plant stops 10 minutes, the company will lose I don't know how many millions of dollars," said Maria Lilia Almaraz, who earns $10.60 an hour cutting bones from cuts of meat with a razor-sharp blade. "It's always, faster, faster," she said.

Deadly Accidents

In July 2000, Jesus Soto Carbajal was cutting rounds of beef from hindquarters coming down the line at him every six seconds near the end of his shift at Excel Corp.'s meatpacking plant in Schuyler, Nebraska. He was working alone on the line; a coworker had left early. An investigative reporter tells what happened:

> No one witnessed the exact moment. Maybe the cuts were taking just that much too long because Soto couldn't pause to sharpen his knife. Maybe the next slab whacked Soto's hand as he turned a beat late.

The wound didn't look that bad. Martin Contreras, still a high-level worker at the plant, had seen gashes gush far more blood. This man will survive, he thought, standing above Soto.

The knife had punctured Soto's chest just above the protective mesh. Above the left collar bone where the jugular vein returns blood from the head to the heart. Within minutes, Soto went from yelling in pain to dazed silence.

Contreras sped behind the ambulance in a manager's car past cornfields and the Last Chance steakhouse to the medical clinic. It turned out there was no need to rush.

The Associated Press report further noted that:

Excel was not fined for Soto's death because no federal safety standards covered the circumstances that killed him, according to the Occupational Safety and Health Administration. . . . A spokesman for Excel, owned by Minneapolis-based Cargill Inc., said the company has outfitted workers with extended safety tunics.

The speed at which hogs are moved through a pork processing plant was described by a Smithfield manager in testimony at an unfair labor practice trial in 1998–1999. The manager testified that at the Tar Heel plant it took "between five and ten minutes" from the instant a hog is first slain to the completion of draining, cleaning, cleaving, kidney-popping, fat-pulling, snap-chilling, and other steps before disassembly.

Look at me now. I'm twenty-two years old, and I feel like an old man.

"The Lines Are Too Fast"

One interviewed worker from Smithfield Foods' Tar Heel plant told Human Rights Watch:

The line is so fast there is no time to sharpen the knife. The knife gets dull and you have to cut harder. That's when it really starts to hurt, and that's when you cut yourself. I cut my hand at the end of my shift, around 10:30 at night. . . . I went to the clinic the next day at 11:00 a.m. They gave me stitches and told me to come back at 2:30 before the start of my shift to check on the stitches. They told me to go back to work at 3:00. I never stopped working.

Poultry processing is even more frenzied. Line workers make more than 20,000 repetitive hard cuts in a day's work. A Mexican woman poultry worker in Northwest Arkansas said:

I came to Arkansas from California in 1994. I started working in chicken lines in 1995. At that time we did thirty-two birds a minute. I took off a year in 1998 when I had a baby. After I came back the line was forty-two birds a minute. People can't take it, always harder, harder, harder [*mas duro, mas duro, mas duro*].

Blood and flesh fall into the meat. The birds just keep going.

Another woman poultry worker said, "The lines are too fast. The speed is for machines, not for people. Maybe we could do it if every cut was easy, but a lot of the chickens are hard to cut. You have to work the knife too hard. That's when injuries happen."

A male worker with swollen hands apparently fixed in claw-like position said:

I hung the live birds on the line. Grab, reach, lift, jerk. Without stopping for hours every day. Only young, strong guys can do it. But after a time, you see what happens. Your arms stick out and your hands are frozen. Look at me now. I'm twenty-two years old, and I feel like an old man. . . .

The force and direction of stabs, cuts, jerks and yanks are unpredictable. "Sometimes it's like butter, sometimes it's like leather," explained one Northwest Arkansas poultry worker interviewed by Human Rights Watch, displaying scars on her hands. "Sometimes the only way to make the cut is toward yourself. Everybody is on top of each other, so a lot of people get cut, especially their hands. Or they stick themselves with injection needles [for marinade injection]. Blood and flesh fall into the meat. The birds just keep going."

Heavy Lifting

Despite advances in automation, many jobs in meatpacking involve lifting, shoving, and turning of heavy animals and animal parts, or of saws and other equipment. In poultry, "live hangers" constantly and rapidly lift bunches of chickens from the ground to overhead hooks to begin the slaughtering and disassembly process. Here is how one analyst described live hang labor:

> Chicken processing is a dirty business, but no job in a poultry plant is more dreaded than "live hang." Here, workers known as "chicken hangers" grab birds by their feet and sling them on to fast-moving metal hooks. This is the first—and dirtiest—stage of poultry processing. The birds, weighing approximately five pounds each, fight back by pecking, biting, and scratching the hangers, who wear plastic cones around their forearms to shield off chicken attacks. Then, as workers finally hoist the birds onto the hooks, the chickens urinate and defecate out of desperation, often hitting the workers below. . . .

[The following is] a Smithfield plant manager's . . . description of hog processing operations at the Tar Heel, North Carolina plant, where workers kill and cut up twenty-five thousand hogs a day. Among other characteristics of the job, the manager said:

Sometimes some of those hogs will go onto the floor, and a hog may need to be pulled to a location where they can be hoisted back onto the line. . . . There is a lot of heavy lifting and repetitive work you know in that environment depending on the weather because it's right there by the livestock area. . . . There are people that tend the scald tub and there are times when hogs become unshackled under the water and the only way to get them out of there is with a long steel hook and pull them to one end and reshackle them back to the line again. That's a difficult job. Heavy lifting, and that is you know always in a hot work environment. . . . When the hog comes out on the other side it comes onto a conveyor belt type table. At that point again another tough job is that the person that works on that gam table depending on how that hog comes out of there is going to have to flip dead weight, flip that hog from one side to the other if he doesn't come out with his feet to the right.

Sullied Work Conditions

Whatever protective equipment they are furnished, workers inevitably come into contact with blood, grease, animal feces, ingesta (food from the animal's digestive system), and other detritus from the animals they slaughter. . . .

Many workers have painful reactions to conditions, but they do not act for fear of losing their jobs. "I am sick at work with a cold and breathing problems, and my arms are always sore," a Smithfield worker said. "I have red rashes on my arms and hands, and the skin between my fingers is dry and cracked. I think I have an allergic reaction to the hogs. But I am afraid to say anything about this because I'm afraid they will fire me."

9

Worker Safety Is a Primary Concern at Food Processing Plants

J. Patrick Boyle

J. Patrick Boyle is the president and CEO of the American Meat Institute, a national trade association representing companies that process 70 percent of U.S. meat and poultry throughout America.

Despite sensational claims by antiagriculture activists such as Human Rights Watch, the working conditions in meatpacking plants are safe. Injury rates have been declining for decades and factory owners have gone to great lengths to ensure that their workers are well-trained about issues of safety. In addition, worker safety is monitored by the Occupational Safety and Health Administration (OSHA), a federal bureau that publishes strict guidelines that meatpackers are obligated to follow. Human Rights Watch ignores these facts and has published a long report about meat processing plants that is as inaccurate as it is irresponsible. The falsehoods and baseless claims put forth by Human Rights Watch are irresponsible and harmful and do a disservice to the well-trained and satisfied workers who thrive in the food processing industry.

The [Human Rights Watch] report alleging harsh working conditions and abusive employment practices in America's meat and poultry processing plants is replete with falsehoods

J. Patrick Boyle, "Human Rights Watch Report 'Way off the Mark,' Says AMI," PRNewswire, January 24, 2005. Reproduced by permission of the American Meat Institute.

and baseless claims. In fact, there are so many refutable claims and irresponsible accusations contained in this 175 page report that it would take another 175 pages to correct the errors.

Among the falsehoods and misleading allegations in the report:

[1.] The report alleges that "meatpacking work has extraordinarily high rates of injury." The meat and poultry industry has seen a significant and consistent decline in injury rates and illnesses for more than a decade. These improvements are extraordinary, particularly in a field where many workers use very sharp knives or work with live or freshly harvested animals. Worker safety and retention has to be a high priority if meatpacking companies want to stay in business. The fact that there are employees who work on the line and have been working in the industry for decades speaks volumes about the environment in which they work.

The report charges meatpackers with "widespread underreporting of injuries." The Occupational Safety and Health Administration (OSHA) closely and regularly monitors the record keeping of employers to ensure that injuries are reported. Major lapses in record keeping would result in citations and fines leveled by OSHA. OSHA has not had a significant complaint against a meatpacker for decades. Workers who are injured on the job receive compensation, and their rights as workers are guaranteed by federal law.

The report claims that workers are forced to work at "unprecedented volume and pace." The report claims that line speeds should be reduced to address "foreseeable and preventable risk of injury," yet the injury rate industry wide is lower than ever. Line speeds, which are monitored by USDA's Food Safety and Inspection Service, have not changed appreciably in 15 years, and are engineered to ensure that the amount of work reaching an employee is appropriate and safe.

[2.] The report claims that "many" workers in the industry are undocumented, and thus easily exploitable. Since 1997, the meatpacking industry has been at the forefront in working with the U.S. Immigration and Naturalization Service (now Citizenship and Immigration Service) to develop, test and implement a program designed to ensure that only those workers who are in the country legally have access to jobs in the meat and poultry industry. Last year, based upon the success of this pilot program, Congress directed that it be expanded nationwide for all types of employers. Instead of exploiting workers, many plants offer English as a Second Language classes and citizenship workshops for employees.

The report accuses the meatpacking industry of taking advantage of the limited ability of some of its employees to speak English. The opposite is true. The meatpacking industry has always been a gateway industry for newly arrived immigrants. Although employees are encouraged to learn English on the job, and some companies offer programs to assist that effort, signs in dominant foreign languages, as well as bilingual supervisors are commonplace in packing plants.

Jobs in the meatpacking industry still pay more than twice the minimum wage.

[3.] The report claims that workers who try to "form unions and bargain collectively" are "suspended, fired, [or] deported." Many workers have decided to remain non-union because they see little value in union membership. Today, only eight (8) percent of non-government employees in the U.S. belong to labor unions. By contrast, meatpacking plants are four times above the national average in union membership. The reason some unions may be unsuccessful in organizing additional meat and poultry facilities is because the workers see little or no value in union membership, given the wages being offered industry wide.

[4.] The report criticizes meatpacking plants for having internal security on staff. Since 9/11, the government has repeatedly warned those in the food industry that bio-terrorism, or attacks against this nation's food supply, is a real and possible threat. Failure to provide adequate security on premises would invite attacks on this nation's food supply. Furthermore, added security makes plants safer for all employees as well.

[5.] The report claims that the "1980s saw the destruction of good jobs in the meatpacking industry." The fact is that jobs in the meatpacking industry still pay more than twice the minimum wage. But when examining total compensation packages, including benefits such as health care and retirement plans, the industry is well above the national average in comparable salaries. Lastly, most meatpacking plants are located in rural areas with generally lower costs of living and generally lower wages than in larger urban areas. This fact should be considered when comparing meatpacking plant wages to national averages.

[6.] The report contains a disclaimer footnote which explains that since it was "not possible" to interview workers in all factories industry-wide, the specific findings of this report "may not apply to all workplaces at all times." With a title like "Blood, Sweat and Fear, Workers Rights in the U.S. Meat and Poultry Plants," the author obviously and intentionally misled readers into assuming that these allegations were applicable industry-wide. This underscores the unreliable nature of the contents of the entire report. In addition, the author implies first-hand knowledge of safety issues in plants which he has never been inside. The "unlawful tactics" cited in one plant are taken from a report first released 8 years ago—hardly applicable today.

The ethnic diversity and longevity of employment of our workers is proof positive that both newcomers and native-born Americans continue to see meatpacking jobs as a viable step toward the American dream. Our commitment to the health, prosperity and happiness of our half million employees can be demonstrated by the tens of thousands of workers who choose to spend their careers in our plants.

10

Genetically Engineered Crops Pose Many Risks

Sally Deneen

Sally Deneen is a Seattle-based freelance writer.

Genetically engineered (GE) ingredients are found in more than half of all processed foods sold in grocery stores. The biotech industry claims that these foods are safe but the presence of genetically engineered molecules in the food chain raises troubling issues. Few studies, for example, have been conducted to determine if biotech crops contain harmful toxins that trigger allergies. Farmers are also concerned that the distribution of GE crops cannot be controlled: Natural forces carry GE species far from where they were originally planted, sometimes contaminating organic crops. Despite the assurances of large agribusiness corporations, GE crops should be treated with suspicion. Consumers should buy organic food whenever possible and shun biotech unless the crops can be reliably regulated and safely controlled.

At a supermarket in the Midwest, Mary Lee Treter passes aisles of shelves stocked with countless products containing genetically engineered ingredients: cereal, muffins, milk, taco shells, frozen pizzas, Hawaiian-grown fresh papayas, hot dogs and soda pop. She notices the labels don't say anything about genetically engineered ingredients.

Coca-Cola, Sprite, Pepsi, Hershey's bars, Campbell's soups, Progresso soups, Quaker rice cakes, frozen dinners by Swanson and Healthy Choice, and cereals by Kellogg's and General Mills are among hundreds of products found to contain genetically engineered ingedients, according to tests conducted by Greenpeace for its "True Food Shopping List." About six out of every ten processed foods Treter could choose to drop in her cart contain genetically modified organisms, such as corn altered to contain its own pesticide in every cell.

Then Treter arrives at the organic foods section, a recent innovation at her local Kroger in Toledo, Ohio. "It's really nice, and I'm impressed," she says. "We don't have a lot of organic food markets in this area. It's a little bit more expensive, and that's a downside."

Organic or Biotech?

How Treter and tens of millions of other consumers spend their money is akin to casting a vote between competing and ascending forms of agriculture: genetically modified foods versus organics. Both expanding industries say their techniques are the best and most sensible way to feed the world's growing population. Both maintain they're sustainable forms of agriculture and lighter on the environment than conventional better-living-through-chemistry agribusiness.

Without labels, the only way consumers can be certain to avoid gene-spliced ingredients is to buy foods from. . . certified organics.

But only genetically altered foods raise concerns from a broad range of scientists, academics and ethicists for developing never-before-seen techniques such as adding jellyfish genes to wheat to make plants glow whenever they need water. Or inserting a bacteria gene into corn to ward off pests. Only biotech foods have sparked a campaign among farmers calling for a moratorium on genetically engineered (GE) wheat, and prompted some parents to campaign against genetically engineered foods in school cafeterias. And significantly, biotech threatens—through overuse—to render useless organics' main defense against pests, a natural pesticide derived from the soil bacterium Bacillus thuringiensis and known as Bt.

Proponents contend that future biotech products such as cancer-fighting tomatoes and vitamin E-enhanced soybeans will do for the 21st century what vitamin-fortified foods did in the 20th century. While the industry makes assurances that GE foods are safe for people and the environment, the world's scientific community has not come to a consensus. U.S. regulators are playing a slow game of catch-up, relying on a gap-filled patchwork of existing regulations to deal with a novel industry. Monsanto is embroiled in lawsuits with farmers over patent matters. Meanwhile, some corn and soybean growers complain that the technology costs too much, bringing them smaller yields and higher costs. And to the frustration of consumers like Treter, politicians can't agree on whether these foods need to be labeled.

Without labels, the only way consumers can be certain to avoid gene-spliced ingredients is to buy foods from the other ascending form of agriculture—certified organics. Of course, organic food may also carry benefits beyond food safety: a 2001 study in the Journal of Alternative and Complementary Medicine found that organic crops had higher average levels of 21 nutrients studied, including vitamin C and iron. Last March, research at the University of California revealed that organic produce may contain more natural antioxidants, which have been linked to reduced risk for cancer, stroke, heart disease and other illnesses.

It's an odd choice: "organic" or "other." Treter absolutely believes GE foods should be labeled and confirms industry fears when she says labels may discourage her from buying: "It would certainly make me think. And it would probably sway me."

Despite industry lobbying against labeling genetically engineered foods, most Americans polled say they overwhelmingly want labels. Yet, they often vote against organics and—often times unwittingly—in favor of GE foods at the checkout line. It is that disconnect that is helping fuel the growth of the biotech food industry.

Increasing Acreage

Since GE crops first became available to farmers in the mid-1990s, they have swelled to more than 145 million acres worldwide by 2002. Seventy percent of today's biotech crops grow in the United States.

It's a trend on the rise: Eighty percent of all soybeans and 70 percent of all cotton now grown in the U.S. are genetically engineered. So is 38 percent of all corn. Corn and soy turn up in processed foods as oils. GE soy binds hot dogs, and ground corn ends up in taco shells and chips. Most corn and soybeans are fed to animals, so consumers likely eat meat and poultry from animals raised on GE feed. Flax, canola, Hawaiian-grown papayas and some squashes are also GE-authorized in the U.S. Wheat is probably next. Down the road could come lettuce, strawberries, sweet potatoes, sugar and allergen-free peanuts, among others. Then there is the next wave of biotech products—transgenic animals and plant-based pharmaceuticals. They include salmon altered to grow faster, tobacco engineered to contain pharmaceuticals for non-Hodgkins lymphoma, and corn altered to contain pharmaceuticals for cystic fibrosis or E. coli sufferers.

Is there reason to worry? Just what are the downsides—and advantages—of GE foods? Monsanto, DuPont and other major players have argued that their biotech foods promise to feed the world while cutting pesticide use and curbing soil erosion. Proponents say future varieties will help people live healthier lives. They'll also save lives in the Third World, thanks to novel foods such as bananas that contain vaccines. . . .

Jane Rissler is among scientists who fear these crops are on the path to becoming self-perpetuating, uncontrollable weeds that outcompete other plants and encourage the development of super pest insects. All the while, consumers will eat unlabeled foods that haven't been subjected to long-term tests or strict government oversight. Whenever you put a foreign gene into food, major concerns arise: Will it trigger an allergic reaction? Will the new genes or proteins produce potentially harmful toxins? So far, the industry and the federal government contend the current varieties of GE foods are safe. Critics concede they don't appear to present a grave risk, but wonder about potentially subtle long-term effects.

"There has not been a systematic study of their safety," says Rissler, a former biotechnology regulator with the U.S. Environmental Protection Agency (EPA) who now works for the Union of Concerned Scientists. "Most people are relying on the absence of evidence to give them comfort. I would prefer that we actually gather evidence. . . . The fact is, people are not looking for evidence of harm."

Besides that, consumers so far have gained nothing from the new technology, Rissler says. "I think the technique introduces a great deal of uncertainty about which we have little experience. Once we have experience, and better data, then we'll have a better idea of the risks," says Rissler.

Safe to Eat?

Right now, there are two dominant types of biotech crops. Three-quarters are herbicide-tolerant plants engineered to thrive after being doused with the weed killer glyphosate, the active ingredient in Monsanto's Roundup. Many other popular crops are engineered so that every cell contains the Bt pesticide.

Three federal agencies rely on largely pre-existing rules to regulate the novel industry. Biotech producers maintain the system is sufficient. For plants that contain their own pesticide to ward off insects, it's the EPA's job to ensure they are safe for the environment. The Department of Agriculture (USDA) gives permits to test new varieties in the field. The Food and Drug Administration (FDA) is to make sure biotech crops are safe for humans or animals to eat.

Trouble is, the FDA relies on a voluntary process to regulate the industry. That is, biotech food developers voluntarily submit summaries of their safety tests for the FDA to review. Using the Freedom of Information Act to obtain records, former EPA scientist Doug Gurian-Sherman and colleagues examined more than a quarter of the 53 so-called "data summaries" that food developers presented to the FDA for review. They noticed a troubling pattern.

"The biotechnology companies provide inadequate data to ensure their products are safe. In addition, it was clear from our review that the FDA performs a less-than-thorough safety analysis," concluded Gurian-Sherman, science director for the Biotechnology Project at the Center for Science in the Public Interest.

In six of the 14 cases studied by Gurian-Sherman, the government asked the biotech-food developer for more information in order to complete a thorough safety assessment—but received answers only in three cases. In case after case, according to his report, "The FDA did not generate its own safety assessment, but merely summarized for the public the developer's analysis." ...

Sacrificial Soy

The safety reports are too late for Gail Wiley, a soybean grower in central North Dakota. She and her husband, Tom, were ready to ship their conventionally grown, food-grade soybeans to Japan in the summer of 2000 when their beans underwent a final test—this time to ensure they weren't genetically engineered. Japan officially allowed only one percent of a shipment to be contaminated with genetically engineered beans.

The test came in at a disappointing 1.37 percent. "So we lost that contract," says Wiley. "We sold the soybeans on the open market, losing about $10,000."

Wiley's farm has 11 neighbors, some growing GE soybeans. "For us to know which neighbor's fields contaminated us would be really difficult. It's impossible to prove where the contamination came from—if it was pollen, if it was bees, if it was wind. It's even hard to find seed that isn't contaminated," says Wiley. . . .

"You cannot build a wall high enough to keep GMOs [genetically modified organisms] out of the environment, as pollen often drifts for miles on the wind, potentially contaminating everything in its path," argues Arran Stephens, president and founder of Nature's Path Foods, maker of organic food products.

Once contaminated, harvested organic crops can't be sold at a premium. While comprising only one percent of the food market, sales of organic foods have grown 20 percent a year for the last nine years, boosting it to a $6 billion industry. The amount of organic cropland and pasture has more than doubled since 1997, bringing the 2001 total to 2.34 million acres in the contiguous U.S.

As demand for organic foods rises, it becomes that much more important for organic farmers to avoid GE contamination. "It's important for people to know that if we don't stop genetic engineering, we're not going to have a thriving system of organic agriculture," contends Simon Harris, national campaign director for the Organic Consumers Association.

There's also a bizarre side effect of the drift phenomenon. Some growers complain that they've been pressured by Monsanto to pay fees to the company after stray gene-altered plants ended up growing on their farms, says farmer advocate Bill Wenzel. Monsanto has sued hundreds of farmers, usually on the grounds of patent infringement. From Monsanto's viewpoint, the company is only protecting its costly investment of developing the novel seeds. When farmers buy Monsanto seeds, they sign agreements to buy new seeds each year. . . .

Why GE?

The promise of bigger profits via bigger yields or lower pesticide costs lures farmers to begin growing GE crops, according to a USDA study. Results are mixed, partly because seed costs are high. Iowa farmers who raised GE soybeans and corn in 1998 and 2000 didn't gain better returns than conventional competitors, according to Iowa State University. By Monsanto's account, its Roundup Ready soybeans reduced herbicide costs for U.S. soybean farmers by almost $700 million between 1997 and 2000.

If foreign countries start turning away American wheat because some portion is genetically engineered, the resulting domestic oversupply could plummet prices paid to farmers by one-third.

All of this leads to the question: Why grow GE? That's simple, proponents say. Some biotech crops are engineered to ward off pests. "Roundup Ready" varieties can be doused with the herbicide and thrive, even as surrounding weeds die. Farmers plant GE corn as sort of an "insurance policy" in fields where pest outbreaks are likely, according to Mike Duffy, an agricultural economist at Iowa State. Soybean growers plant biotech varieties in hopes of easier, faster harvests. Duffy found they especially have incentive to use GE seeds if they're renting farmland from landlords who want clean-looking, weed-free fields.

There are some tangible benefits to growers. "Farmers are, at least, not being disadvantaged" by growing GE crops, according to a 2002 USDA report. "Farmers are not stupid. They're not going to buy something that won't give them a return," says Lisa Dry, spokesperson for the Biotechnology Industry Organization.

Most genetically modified seeds worldwide are controlled by a few corporations, including Syngenta, Monsanto, DuPont and Aventis. The American Corn Growers Association has complained that such concentration is dangerous. That's because they're not just seed companies. They develop relationships with firms involved with producing and processing food, which means they maintain control from the seed to supermarket, notes Bill Heffernan, professor emeritus of rural sociology at the University of Missouri-Columbia.

Family farmers are hit hard by a more immediate problem—the loss of overseas markets. From Austria to Zimbabwe, many people mistrust genetically engineered foods. Protesters in the United Kingdom have trampled fields of gene-altered corn. Forty-four to 70 percent of Europeans disapprove of so-called "Frankenfoods," surveys show.

U.S. corn growers . . . lost more than $814 million in foreign sales [between 1998 and 2003] as a result of restrictions on genetically modified food imports imposed by Europe, Japan and other world buyers, according to the American Corn Growers Association. The implications for U.S. wheat farmers could be huge, according to Robert Wisner, an economics professor at Iowa State. If foreign countries start turning away American wheat because some portion is genetically engineered, the resulting domestic oversupply could plummet prices paid to farmers by one-third, Wisner testified to the Montana legislature. By his reckoning, the nation has lost more than $1 billion in corn and soybean meal exports because of foreign concerns.

In September [2002], American Corn Growers' Association CEO Larry Mitchell called for Congress to study the cost of genetically engineered crops—not only to corn growers, but also to taxpayers, who had to offset $5.4 billion of loans because of lost farm income in 2001. "We need to know the cost of lost export markets, lower corn prices and higher seed prices," Mitchell says. In short, whether you like GE foods or not, you're helping pay for them. . . .

In the end, what is a consumer to do? If you want to avoid GE foods, buy or grow your own certified organic alternatives. You can also make home-cooked meals with locally grown ingredients instead of relying on big-brand prepared foods. So far, supermarket vegetables and fruits aren't genetically engineered, save for some papayas and squash. If you're OK with GE foods, do nothing at all. You're eating them already.

11

Genetically Engineered Crops Have Provided Great Benefits to the World

International Foundation for the Conservation of Natural Resources

The International Foundation for the Conservation of Natural Resources (IFCNR) is a global advocate of the biotechology industry.

Genetically modified (GM) crops are currently growing in countries across the globe. The food from these crops feeds hundreds of millions of people and presents one of the greatest success stories in agricultural history. The motives of environmental groups and other nongovernmental organizations (NGOs) that have issued dire warnings about GM crops are questionable because many of them have ties to the multibillion-dollar organic food industry. Others are simply anti-capitalist or anti-American and seem to care more about nature than they do about those who are starving. While these environmentalists raise millions of dollars to campaign against GM crops, people in developing nations go hungry. Thankfully, farmers have not been swayed by environmentalist propaganda and continue to plant genetically modified crops so that they can feed the world.

Over the echoing protests of anti-GMO critics like Friends of the Earth, Greenpeace and other crusading environmental groups, farmers around the world exercised their opin-

International Foundation for the Conservation of Natural Resources, "While Greenpeace Protests, Farmers Opt for GM Crops," ifcnr.com, May 11, 2005. Reproduced by permission.

ion of biotech agriculture by planting the billionth acre with genetically enhanced seeds, an event marked by agricultural analysts as occurring May 8th [2005].

For a world historically resistant to change, the acceptance of genetically modified crops by the world's agricultural community is nothing short of astounding. A billion acres consisting largely of genetically enhanced soya, corn, cotton, and canola planted by some eight million farmers in 17 countries worldwide now populate the earth after a scant decade after the commercial debut of the science of applied agricultural biotechnology.

The safety and palatability of genetically modified foods lies in the fact that for more than eight years not a single case of adverse health effects have come from the more than 300 million consumers of genetically modified foods.

Crops developed by means of applied agricultural genetics reduce cost and labor for farmers. Crop yield improves. Environment destroying chemical pesticides use is reduced. The potential for eliminating crop disease is now a question of process not theory. Perhaps the profound effect of farming GMO crops is on those living closest to the land in impoverished locales whose agricultural efforts proved hitherto unyielding in productivity or profit. Fully a third of all GMO crops are planted by farmers in economically developing nations.

According to the Food and Agriculture Organization (FAO) of the United Nations, a sizeable number of developing nations led by Argentina, Brazil, China, Cuba, Egypt, India, Mexico, and South Africa are not only opting to plant GMO crops developed by international life science firms in the United States and Europe, they are also in the research and development arena seeking to find hybrids suitable to local environs through genetics. Among the crops being investigated are crops with disease-resistant characteristics as well as those that can tolerate growing conditions hampered by soil salinity and atmospheric drought. Among those crops are new variants of papaya, sweet potatoes, cassava, rice, bananas, cowpeas, plantains and sorghum.

An Outspoken Bias

Just why applied agricultural genetics rubs environmental and animal rights groups in such a negative way may be explained, in part, by the profit potential.

Masking a decidedly hypocritical view of the root motivation for capitalism "profit" behind the claim that humankind is using science to create unnatural organisms, GMO critics seem loath to allow anyone to profit nutritionally, intellectually, or financially from the fruits of modern agriculture.

Their outspoken bias against genetic manipulation is an intellectual canard. Tinkering with the genetics of food crops, food animals, pets and even our own offspring has been a willful preoccupation of humans since first our ancestors stood upright. We've taken the barely edible kernels of Central American teosinte grass and coaxed it via genetics into what we know today as corn or maize. The plump purple eggplants so admired by "organic" farmers and consumers had its genes mixed and matched from it origin as the small round white globes grown in India. Selective breeding not only produced 190 plus "pure" dog breeds and countless mutt variants from wolves, it also accounts for the physical traits of children common to certain geographical regions, traits developed by the preferential mating among humans.

Leaders of the environmental and animal rights movements must know this. Collectively they are among the most intelligent of society's brood and undoubtedly were exposed to at minimum a passing acquaintance with basic genetics from science classes taught grade school through postgraduate education, unless of course, they are among the intellectually gifted who simply failed to pay attention in class.

Cries of alarm over human consumption of alien GMO genes are equally contrived. As GMO advocates point out, and quite correctly so, humans consume foreign genes from the panoply of foodstuffs we dine upon daily: genes from beef, pork, chicken, fish, and every variety of fruit and vegetable. DNA, whether from GMO maize or wild salmon, is broken down by the digestive process. If consumption of non-human DNA was the means of incorporating new genetic material in humans, circumpolar inhabitants would have grown gills, scales, fins, or flippers long ago.

Many anti-GMO groups at the forefront of the activist ramparts have direct financial ties to the organic food industry.

Economic Hypocrisy

A close look at the campaigns waged against GMOs reveals a substrata of staunch anti-capitalist and anti-globalization ideology liberally laced with economic hypocrisy.

In one sense, the anti-GMO stance against capitalism cleverly plays to the consumer/workforce bias against cold, impersonal, faceless corporations. Targeting international corporations like the USA's Monsanto or Switzerland's Syngenta makes sense from a PR strategy point of view. It creates a "David versus Goliath" scenario tailored to winning sympathy for feisty little NGO activists battling global corporate giants. By narrowing the anti-GMO fight on a firm such as Monsanto plays to the nationalistic jealousy and insecurity that fans the flames of anti-Americanism around the world.

Where GMO crops are proving their worth by allowing poverty-stricken hardscrabble farmers in India and Africa to feed their families, supply local nutritional needs, and finally turn a modest profit on their crops, the anti-capitalist/anti-America card is quick to be played. Firms like Monsanto are pilloried for charging for seeds. The news headlines fed by activist press statements decry "America bullies local farmers!"

Anti-GMO hypocrisy is rampant. Many anti-GMO groups at the forefront of the activist ramparts have direct financial ties to the organic food industry. As organic producers grow in profitability so too do their "marketing" strategists. In addition, the very groups that condemn a Monsanto or Syngenta for "selling" their wares in hopes of turning a profit are fast to pass the fundraising basket to keep millions flowing into their bank accounts. Their proliferation of tee shirts with catchy protest slogans and cut-glass stemware etched with a fetching panda or whale for sale via on-line catalogues aren't given away gratis.

Compassion for animals and the earth apparently does not extend to compassion for the hungry and ill humans cohabitating with exotic wildlife. If crops tilled the "organic" way fail and GMO crops thrive, the impoverished Third World farmer is expected to remain ideologically pure while his family starves. Animal rights extremists harbor not so secret hopes that failure equals evacuation of humans from wildlife habitat. Fewer humans, more animals is their mantra.

Friends of the Earth and Greenpeace may hold sway over how some perceive GMO foods, but those groups do not contribute the first bushel of corn or potatoes or pound of meat or fish to the world food supply. Farmers do. Farmers therefore are in a far better position to determine the course of global food production. More and more the world's farmers choose GMO and rightly so.

12

Shrimp Farms Have Disastrous Effects on People and the Environment

Public Citizen

Public Citizen is a national, nonprofit consumer advocacy organization founded in 1971 to represent consumer interests in Congress, the executive branch, and the courts.

Those who farm fish and shellfish in developing nations are causing widespread environmental pollution and using inefficient methods of factory aquaculture. Developing nations need sustainable aquaculture to feed their own citizens, but they are instead farming cheap shrimp that is exported to the United States and other wealthy countries. In the process aquaculturists pollute huge quantities of water with chemicals and fish waste before dumping it back into oceans and streams. Meanwhile, those who live nearby are denied sufficient, clean water necessary to grow rice and other crops. Industrial shrimp farms are destroying large swaths of the coastline where people depend on the seas for food. Americans should not eat factory farmed shrimp because it is bad for the environment and hurts poor farm families struggling to survive in the developing world.

Aquaculture is the farming of aquatic organisms, including fish, mollusks, crustaceans and aquatic plants. Like all farming, it involves some form of intervention in the rearing

Public Citizen, "Shell Game: The Environmental and Social Impacts of Shrimp Aquaculture," citizen.org, 2005. This report was originally produced by the Shrimp Campaign of Public Citizen's Critical Mass, Energy and Environmental Program. In November 2005, this campaign moved to a new organization called Food & Water Watch, which is reproducing this report with Public Citizen's permission.

process to enhance production, such as regular stocking, feeding, and protection from predators. Aquaculture can be done in inland freshwater environments and in or adjacent to the sea. Done for the right purposes and in the right manner, aquaculture offers the potential to bolster local food security and livelihood opportunities for many of the one-billion people in the world who suffer greatly from the lack of both.

Many consumers in the U.S., Japan, and Europe want to understand more about the effects their consumption is having on others around the world. The story of farmed shrimp is also one that health conscious consumers might want to hear, because if they knew more about what might be lurking in the flesh of farmed shrimp, they might think twice about eating too much of it, or about eating any at all. Consumers have a right to know all about the health risks and environmental and social costs associated with the food they eat.

Shrimp aquaculture is also a story that the seafood trade and marketing industry doesn't want consumers to know. Naturally enough, companies engaged in the seafood marketing industry have been making fortunes off of cheap farm-raised shrimp and they don't want any negative publicity. Some companies have formed a well-funded *shrimp task force* of corporations who are *"fighting for America's #1 seafood."* But, cheap shrimp is bad shrimp. The reason why shrimp is cheaper today than it has ever been is because the true costs of producing it has been and continues to be paid for by the environment and the rural communities in the Global South, not by the consumers.

Environmental Costs

Diverse natural landscapes have been, and are still being, radically transformed into vast monoculture cropping systems called "shrimp farms" laid out for as far as the eye can see. The wide array of negative environmental impacts created by shrimp aquaculture expansion has been well documented in an exhaustive list of studies spanning two decades. Aside from the well-documented environmental impacts, the industrialized production of shrimp imposes socio-economic costs on communities as their traditional means of food production and livelihoods are displaced.

All forms of aquaculture—such as shrimp and salmon—affect biodiversity by degrading habitat, disrupting trophic systems, transmitting diseases and reducing genetic variability. The best-known example of habitat alteration is the impact of shrimp farming on mangrove ecosystems. These coastal forests encompass very high species diversity both in the water and on adjacent lands. In Southeast Asia they contribute about one-third of yearly landings of wild fish. From the late-1970s, an estimated 2.5 million to 3.75 million acres (1 to 1.5 million hectares) of various types of coastal wetland environments, including salt flats, marshes, and mangrove forests, were cleared away by bulldozers to construct shrimp production complexes, along with additional lands used for subsistence agricultural purposes, such as growing rice.

Because of the need for brackish water and the grave misconception that mangroves are wastelands of little economic value, shrimp farm investors predominantly settled in these coastal forests to cut costs. But, mangrove ecosystems provide an abundance of services to communities that have been fulfilling their needs for centuries. In addition, mangroves support the functioning of other ecosystems in the seascape, such as coral reef ecosystems further offshore. Shrimp farming development that destroys mangroves, and other related wetlands, therefore translates into environmental and social costs, which are not paid for by the industry, nor by consumers of shrimp in foreign markets. Several studies have addressed the environmental and social values of mangroves, but those values are never accounted for when calculating the true costs of shrimp farming; thus, short-sighted and narrow economic analyses make it appear that shrimp farms provide more economic worth than mangroves, which, as in Thailand, is not the case.

Converting tidal wetlands for shrimp farms and building roads, dykes, and canals to service the farms threatens biodiversity in the tropics, particularly in Latin America and Southeast Asia. Tidal marshes and mangroves that serve as nursery grounds for marine life are lost through the conversion process. The destruction of wetlands has caused dramatic declines in biodiversity, with impacts felt far beyond the immediate targeted area, for example, on migratory birds that use the ecosystems at various stages of their life cycles. Wild populations of fish and shrimp decline. Such impacts on fish stocks and other sea creatures, even wild populations of shrimp, inevitably lead to reduced fish catches for local fisherfolk. . . .

It takes several pounds of wild fish to produce enough fishmeal to grow just one pound of shrimp for the market—a highly wasteful practice with serious implications for the preservation of marine biodiversity.

Ecological Footprint in the Sand

The millions of acres of wetlands and agriculture lands converted to shrimp farms reflect only *part* of the negative environmental impacts and damage done to subsistence-based communities. Each acre of a shrimp farm can require as much as 200 additional "shadow acres" of ecosystems for absorbing the ecological costs of factory farming of shrimp. For example, researchers investigating shrimp farming in Colombia found that a "farmed" acre required the productive and/or assimilative capacity of as much as 187 acres of additional ecosystems per year.

These "shadow acres" make up the "ecological footprint" of factory-style shrimp farming. This is the area required to supply resources to and absorb the waste from shrimp farming. A shrimp farm requires a vast array of inputs, such as shrimp fry to "seed" the farm, fishmeal to feed the growing shrimp, fertilizers, chemical compounds, and enormous amounts of saline and fresh water. Then, there's the problem of how to dispose of the tons of polluted water and waste products created by shrimp farming—pollutants that are simply discharged onto surrounding lands and into nearby waterways.

How the industrial shrimp aquaculture industry handles feed requirements provides a good example of the ecological footprint left by factory shrimp farming. To grow quickly in captivity, shrimp are fed fishmeal made from fish caught by factory fishing fleets at sea. It takes several pounds of wild fish to produce enough fishmeal to grow just one pound of shrimp for the market—a highly wasteful practice with serious implications for the preservation of marine biodiversity. In fact, this type of fishing practice is a global phenomenon; annually, 30 to 35 million tons, about one-third of the entire global marine fish catch, is reduced to fishmeal and fish oils that is fed to farmed shrimp and salmon, cattle, pigs, chickens and the like.

Shrimp farming requires between 8 and 16 million gallons of salt, brackish, and fresh water in varying proportions to produce just one ton of shrimp.

... and In the Water

One of the most devastating aspects of the enormous ecological footprint of shrimp aquaculture is left on water. If water is life, then shrimp farming is the grim reaper slashing its deadly scythe into the very wellspring of life that sustains human communities everywhere. The impacts on water resources, especially on freshwater supplies, in areas where shrimp aquaculture dominate the landscape are staggering in terms of their extent and magnitude. Depletion, salinization, and chemical pollution of drinking water directly affect villages in areas where shrimp farming dominates the landscape. What it does to water through pollution and massive water use makes shrimp aquaculture a deadly threat to the survival of communities in regions of the world where obtaining clean, potable water is already an overwhelming challenge.

By its very nature, aquaculture generally requires considerably more water than any other industrial process. Shrimp are grown in brackish water ponds in which the water must be continuously renewed and the salinity constantly adjusted in a suitable range. Up to 40% of the water in shrimp ponds are flushed out on a daily basis. The volumes of water used—sea, brackish, and fresh water—are of staggering proportions. Altogether, shrimp farming requires between 8 and 16 million gallons of salt, brackish, and fresh water in varying proportions to produce just one ton of shrimp, or an average of 20 Olympic size swimming pools per ton.

Of great concern is the enormous and unsustainable demand on freshwater supplies that shrimp aquaculture places on communities—the water they need for domestic use and food production. Freshwater must be mixed with highly saline sea water, because shrimp grow best in brackish water at certain stages of their lives. For example, an investigation of shrimp farming in Vietnam done by the Vietnamese Institute for Economics and Marine Planning offers compelling evidence that shrimp aquaculture is not sustainable because of its high demand on freshwater supplies. According to the research report, freshwater is used at a rate of about 5.3 million gallons a year per acre of shrimp farm in the area of Vietnam studied (50,000 cubic meters per hectare). Extrapolating from this, Vietnam's 1.25 million acres (500,000 hectares) of shrimp farms, would consume 210 billion barrels (25 billion cubic meters) of freshwater annually. The report emphasized that tapping fresh water resources in this way is not sustainable, particularly along coastal sandy areas where fresh water resources are limited, which means that the local communities in surrounding areas that depend on the same water for their daily water needs and agricultural production are doomed.

Groundwater extraction of such magnitude for shrimp production not only depletes the resource directly, but as the aquifers are pumped dry, saltwater seeps in from the nearby sea causing salinization. Waste water pumped out of the shrimp farms back into the environment also causes salinization, in addition to pollution of ground water and local lakes and waterways. Saltwater seepage from unlined shrimp ponds adds to the salinity of underground aquifers. Altogether, through direct extraction coupled with salinization, water supplies for domestic needs are destroyed and, to compound the misery, surrounding agricultural lands become salty, making any alternative cropping (such as rice) virtually impossible. Thus, water and food are jeopardized.

Adding to the problems created by the direct extraction of water for shrimp ponds and salinization of surrounding land and waters are pollutants generated through shrimp farming that end up in the surrounding environment. To maintain the overcrowded shrimp population in farms, and to attain higher production efficiency, copious amounts of artificial feed, pesticides, chemical additives, and antibiotics must be continuously added to the aquaculture systems - all eventually end up being purged from the farms and dumped onto surrounding water and land areas. Such wastes include solid matter (eroded pond soils), organics (uneaten, rotting shrimp feed, shrimp feces, dead shrimp, dead plankton) and dissolved metabolites (ammonia, urea and carbon dioxide). Unfortunately, for the many chemical compounds, antibiotics and other therapeutants, some quite toxic, which are widely used in large-scale shrimp farming, accurate statistics on usage are almost nonexistent due to the lack of government monitoring and controls.

These compounds together make the solid and liquid wastes from the ponds potentially quite hazardous to people living in surrounding communities. The polluted liquid wastes are pumped back into the surrounding environment. Any solid wastes remaining at the bottom of the ponds, are dredged out and hauled away to be dumped in other areas where they poison coastal waterways, estuaries, bays, fresh groundwater supplies, native flora and fauna, and adjacent human communities. The recent study in Vietnam by the Vietnamese Institute for Economics and Marine Planning found that each hectare of shrimp farms (1 hectare = 2.5 acres) produces eight tons of solid waste per year. Almost all Vietnamese shrimp farmers dump these solid wastes directly into the ocean, polluting the sea water along coastal areas. Altogether, Vietnam's 1.25 million acres of shrimp farms are adding to the pollution burden of coastal areas by some 6.7 million tons of solid waste annually, according to the Institute's report. In addition, it described how shrimp farmers commonly discharged their polluted waste waters straight into surrounding areas, causing the supplies of potable underground water, creeks and ponds to become brackish and polluted. The report noted that shrimp diseases are also spread from pond to pond this way throughout Vietnam.

Severe Side Effects

Impacts on the health of people living around shrimp farms who are exposed to the chemicals, antibiotics, and other potentially hazardous compounds in the waste water and sludge are evident. Community leaders have for years been reporting how local people, especially children, typically complain about unexplained, unusual symptoms showing up, including sore throats, burning eyes, and skin rashes. Unfortunately, the precise causes of these symptoms and how they might be related to shrimp farming pollution remain undetermined, because no long term studies have been done. The pollution of freshwater wells and aquifers from shrimp farming has other severe side effects for local people: it impacts their food supplies and subsistence economies. The intrusion of salt-water and pollution into local ground water and agricultural areas degrades local supplies of fresh, potable water and the soils used for agricultural food production. In addition, the dumping of vast quantities of polluted solid waste sediments that accumulate in the bottoms of shrimp ponds contributes to the salinity and toxicity in receiving soils and waters. As a consequence of this pollution and salinization, essential food crops—such as rice and vegetables—that need healthy soils and fresh water often become impossible to grow and when they do are contaminated.

In India, Bangladesh, Vietnam, Malaysia, and other rice dependent countries lands that once produced rice enough to feed thousands of families each year, have been either taken over or destroyed by shrimp farms.

The excessive water use by shrimp farms creates numerous other problems. For example, the over-extraction of groundwater by shrimp farmers has contributed to coastal land subsidence, with land sometimes sinking as deep as six feet. Abstraction of freshwater for shrimp culture also uses a lot of energy for pumping and leads to conflicts with other energy and water resources users. As fresh water supplies, energy and other resources for community needs are siphoned away, local people lose what they need for domestic purposes, especially for rice farming.

This happened in Thailand during the 1990s when, because of self-generated pollution and spreading shrimp disease infestations, shrimp farms covering almost a quarter of a million acres along the coast of Thailand collapsed. With no more mangroves left to occupy after having destroyed most of them, shrimp investors pulled up stakes and moved further inland into the country's rice-producing areas where they took up 'low-salinity' shrimp farming. This type of farming was particularly thirsty for fresh water, and soon a fight between traditional rice farmers and the invading shrimp entrepreneurs had begun.

To illustrate the degree of competition for water, a team of Canadian researchers found that in the case of Thai shrimp farming in rice producing areas it takes almost twice the amount of fresh water to produce a pound of shrimp as it does to grow a pound of rice—660 gallons per pound of rice compared to 1,125 gallons of freshwater for a pound of shrimp. Since shrimp is far more profitable, the traditional rice farmers lose out to the new wave of shrimp entrepreneurs. When shrimp farms replace rice fields there is an absolute decrease in the number of jobs available in that area, but perhaps even more devastating, local food needs are denied. In India, Bangladesh, Vietnam, Malaysia, and other rice dependent countries lands that once produced rice enough to feed thousands of families each year, have been either taken over or destroyed by shrimp farms. . . .

Money and other resources that could have been made available for environmentally sound fish aquaculture to feed hungry local markets have been instead diverted to shrimp farming expansion for export markets.

Shrimp for Rich People in Faraway Lands

As mangroves are converted to shrimp ponds, communal land with multi-purpose use becomes private land for single purpose use, controlled by those with political clout and economic capital to gain the land concession from the government. Furthermore, as lands formerly used to produce other staple foods, such as rice, disappear, so do the people's traditional sources of food and income. Local fresh water supplies for drinking and irrigation are usurped by the shrimp industry which needs vast and unceasing amounts to freshen up the water in their shrimp farms. All the while they are pumping back poisonous water and sludges full of toxic chemical wastes, shrimp feces, antibiotics, and other unsavory compounds that infect the surrounding waterways and freshwater wells and aquifers. Poisoned waters hit the children first who start to display symptoms of un-diagnosable, chronic illnesses and other disease symptoms like unprecedented and inexplicable outbreaks of sore throats, eye irritations and skin rashes.

While the waterways and land that coastal communities have used for centuries to catch fish, gather shellfish, grow vegetables and produce rice are taken over by the shrimp industry to produce shrimp for rich people in far away lands, local needs for wholesome nutrition are ignored. Money and other resources that could have been made available for environmentally sound fish aquaculture to feed hungry local markets have been instead diverted to shrimp farming expansion for export markets. As shrimp culture has gained priority in the planning of government departments and international development assistance organizations, such as the World Bank Group, which claims its purpose is to reduce poverty, communities have lost their sources of clean, abundant food and water, and begun to suffer and disintegrate. Altogether, this is real impoverishment.

This is what happens when governments in shrimp producing countries do a policy U-turn from supporting food production for local needs to an export-oriented production policy to produce high-value luxuries, like shrimp. Ironically, the policy shift is advocated on the grounds that it promotes food security. According to the perverse logic of this theory being pedaled by the World Bank, the UN Food and Agriculture Organization, and the multi-national companies making money from shrimp farming, export earnings are supposed to pay for substitute food imports, which are then supposed to somehow 'trickle down' to those in need. In truth, a trickle is about all the nutritionally needy will ever get, since they cannot afford to pay for expensive imported foods. Activists from communities devastated by shrimp farming strenuously reject this imported food substitutes theory. They argue, instead, that export-oriented agriculture reduces food security by encouraging a shift from small-scale, sustainable production to large-scale, non-sustainable industrialized modes of production. It also brings changes in ownership over natural resources and the means of production, from small autonomous producer/owners to large corporate and commercial interests. Peasants are displaced from farming and denied traditional access to land, water and associated natural resources, while commercial interests take over for industrial-scale production of export commodities such as shrimp. These changes are compounded by the negative environmental impacts they generate in production, which cause further hardship for local communities.

13

Fish Farms Are Necessary to Feed a Growing Population

Hauke L. Kite-Powell

Hauke L. Kite-Powell conducts research concerning the economics and management of marine industries and resources, fisheries, and aquaculture at Woods Hole Oceanographic Institution in Massachusetts.

Billions of people depend on fish as one of the main sources of protein in their diet even as wild fish stocks in the ocean are becoming seriously depleted. The only solution to this problem is to raise fish through aquaculture on commercial fish farms. In developing nations, aquaculture provides food, jobs, and money for those in desperate need. In the United States and other industrialized nations, farm-grown fish provides healthful and inexpensive food. Although there are problems associated with aquaculture there is little doubt that it is going be feeding an increasing number of people in the future. Without fish farms, people in developing nations will starve.

Imagine for a moment that the beef and poultry in your refrigerator came not from ranches and farms, but from the woods and prairies. Imagine that every pig, chicken, turkey, and steer was "free range," hunted from wild herds and brought to market. What would that mean to you as a consumer?

In the simplest terms, it would mean that your local supermarket would have higher prices and a less dependable and less plentiful supply of meat. The idea of abandoning our modern practice of raising livestock and harvesting all of our meat from the wild is absurd.

And yet that is exactly how we obtained most of our seafood until quite recently.

Aquaculture, or fish farming, is changing how we think about one of our main sources of protein. With many fish stocks shrinking due to overfishing or environmental degradation, aquaculture holds the promise of more reliable and more sustainable seafood production. The economic and social benefits could be significant for both consumers and producers. . . .

Thanks to the development of aquaculture . . . , the per capita supply of fish has remained roughly constant since 1970.

A New Wave in the Seafood Industry

In 1950, about 20 million tons of fish were harvested globally, with nearly all of that catch coming from wild stocks in oceans, bays, lakes, and rivers. In the five decades since then, the world's population has tripled. Today, seafood production stands at 130 million tons per year, with one quarter of that total coming from aquaculture. About 20 million tons are farmed in freshwater facilities, 15 million tons in salt water.

Aquaculture first began to contribute significantly to world production in the 1970s, when it became clear that wild capture seafood harvests could no longer keep pace with the demand for fish. Many popular fish stocks had been overexploited even before that era, but the fishing industry compensated by repeatedly switching to previously "underutilized" species. By the 1980s, even diversifying the wild harvest could not increase the yield enough to feed the world's booming population and growing appetite.

Humans directly consume 75 percent of all seafood produced, with the remainder being processed into fish meal and oil for use in feeds for land animals and farmed fish. Thanks to the development of aquaculture—output has increased more than fourfold since 1985—the per capita supply of fish has remained roughly constant since 1970.

Seafood accounts for about 15 percent of the protein in the average human diet, about 16 kilograms per person per year. Residents of the United States, however, consume 7 or 8 kilograms per person, about half the global average. When they do eat seafood, few U.S. consumers realize that more than half of what they eat comes from fish farms.

Developing Countries Outpace U.S.

By global standards, U.S. aquaculture production is relatively modest, with a value of less than $1 billion per year of the worldwide total of $50 billion. Catfish, salmon, and oyster farms dominate the U.S. efforts. Aquaculture development is constrained by economics, especially competition from low-wage foreign producers and a lack of available and affordable coastal real estate. As a result, the U.S. imports more than half of the seafood it consumes.

At the other extreme, China accounts for more than half of world aquaculture production, primarily through its large production of freshwater carp, the world's most plentiful aquaculture crop. (There are grounds for suspecting that the Chinese production statistics may be inflated.) Other significant crops include shrimp (tiger prawns) grown in coastal ponds, and seaweeds, oysters, mussels, and salmon grown in ocean cages.

Global aquaculture has focused on species that command a relatively high price. The freedom to select target species is greater for the fish farmer than for the wild capture fisher, and farmers have been selling their products for about $1.50 per kilogram, nearly twice the average price of wild capture seafood. That is good news for the developing world, where aquaculture can feed populations both directly and through income from exports.

Fish in a Barrel

The most common technique for farming fish is pond culture, where fish are reared in shallow, earthen, open-air ponds that look like flooded agricultural fields. This method is mostly used to grow carp and other freshwater fish in Asia, shrimp in Latin America and Asia, and catfish in the southern United States. The simplest ponds are "self-contained" ecosystems in which fish feed on naturally occurring water plants. The density of fish stocked in these ponds is generally low—about 1 kilogram per cubic meter of water—but can be increased with investment in feed and in aeration systems that maintain oxygen levels in the water.

A higher stocking density can be achieved in ocean cage cultures (10 to 20 kilograms per cubic meter), where cages or "netpens" are anchored to the seafloor in open waters. This approach is often used for raising carnivorous marine species such as salmon. Natural currents remove waste products and maintain oxygen levels by continually replacing the water in the cages.

The highest densities are achieved in onshore tank farms, where up to 100 kilograms of fish are raised per cubic meter. These industrial style aquaculture methods use pipes, filters, and flushing systems to remove wastes and restore oxygen levels. Onshore systems rely on regular water exchanges—replacing tank water with fresh water from an external supply—or they circulate the tank water through systems of filters and other water quality systems. . . .

Necessity and Invention

On the island of Zanzibar, in the Indian Ocean off Tanzania, seafood is not a luxury but a means of survival. It is the dominant source of protein for the island's one million residents, who consume three to four times as much seafood as the average New Englander. As in the North Atlantic, many wild capture fish stocks are under intense pressure or depleted, and the catch today is half of what it was 20 years ago. But unlike New Englanders, the people of Zanzibar cannot afford to import fish. The per capita income is about $300 per year.

Aquaculture is critical for the food supply and for economic development of this island. Zanzibar developed a successful seaweed farming industry in the 1980s, and that crop is now second only to tourism in the island's export trades. Seaweed is a source of carrageenan, a key ingredient in the cosmetics, manufactured foods, and pharmaceuticals industries.

This success has spurred interest in other kinds of aquaculture, such as pond farming of finfish and the addition of shellfish to the seaweed plots in coastal lagoons. Limited infrastructure—unreliable utilities and scarce materials—and the lack of a reliable source of juvenile fish have slowed these efforts. So, too, have concerns about environmental degradation . . . which could threaten the island's vital tourism business. . . .

Scientists in Zanzibar are developing a research and training infrastructure to meet these challenges. They have focused on pond culture using low-technology solutions, such as tidal flow instead of pumps for water exchange. They are working with "biofilters," using shellfish and seaweeds to remove excess nutrients from pond water before returning it to the sea. Cage culture experiments in protected nearshore waters are also being planned, and work is starting on a simple hatchery to provide juvenile fish for stocking. Researchers are also developing techniques to add shellfish farming to established seaweed plots.

Initial results from pond culture experiments are promising, and scientists on Zanzibar have begun to instruct would-be fish farmers in how to replicate the experimental farms. The hope is that farmed fish will soon increase the supply of seafood protein available to the residents of the island.

Aquaculture holds great promise, especially in developing countries and historically non-productive coastal areas with few natural wild fish stocks.

Beating Hooks into Plowshares

Aquaculture holds great promise, especially in developing countries and historically non-productive coastal areas with few natural wild fish stocks. Negative environmental effects from poor planning, design, and operating procedures have in some cases been problematic, but can be avoided through sensible regulation and monitoring. In the U.S., automation and other technologies will have to be harnessed to compensate for higher labor costs.

But from a global protein perspective, aquaculture is necessary. The question is not whether to farm fish, but how and where.

14

Industrialized Poultry Farms Are Breeding Grounds for Avian Influenza

Wendy Orent

Wendy Orent is an anthropologist with a special interest in pandemics, a science writer for the Washington Post, *and the author of* Plague: The Mysterious Past and Terrifying Future of the World's Most Dangerous Disease.

Avian influenza, commonly known as bird flu, is a product of the modern factory farm, a system developed in the West and exported to the East in the past thirty years. In Thailand, China, and other Asian nations huge corporate producers pack millions of chickens together in tightly confined quarters. The avian influenza virus first emerged in these industrial farms and spread to the backyards of rural, impoverished Asians who depend on homegrown chickens to ward off starvation. The poultry industry is trying to deflect responsibility for disseminating the virus by blaming wild birds for the epidemic, but factory farms are central to the problem and the most vulnerable citizens in the poorest nations are paying the price for cheap industrialized chicken.

Chicken has never been cheaper. A whole one can be bought for little more than the price of a Starbucks cup of coffee. But the industrial farming methods that make ever-cheaper chicken possible may also have created the lethal strain of bird flu virus, H5N1, that threatens to set off a global pandemic.

According to Earl Brown, a University of Ottawa flu virologist, lethal bird flu is entirely man-made, first evolving in commercially produced poultry in Italy in 1878. The highly pathogenic H5N1 is descended from a strain that first appeared in Scotland in 1959.

People have been living with backyard flocks of poultry since the dawn of civilization. But it wasn't until poultry production became modernized, and birds were raised in much larger numbers and concentrations, that a virulent bird flu evolved. When birds are packed close together, any brakes on virulence are off. Birds struck with a fatal illness can still easily pass the disease to others, through direct contact or through fecal matter, and lethal strains can evolve. Somehow, the virus that arose in Scotland found its way to China, where, as H5N1, it has been raging for more than a decade.

Factory Farms in Asia

Industrial poultry-raising moved from the West to Asia in the last few decades and has begun to supplant backyard flocks there. According to a recent report by Grain, an international nongovernmental organization, chicken production in Southeast Asia has jumped eightfold in 30 years to about 2.7 million tons. The Chinese annually produce about 10 million tons of chickens. Some of China's factory farms raise 5 million birds at a time. Charoen Pokphand Group [C.P. Group], a huge Thai enterprise that owns a large chunk of poultry production throughout Thailand and China as well as in Indonesia, Cambodia, Vietnam and Turkey, exported about 270 million chickens in 2003 alone.

Since then, the C.P. Group, which styles itself as the "Kitchen of the World," has suffered enormous losses from bird flu. According to bird-flu expert Gary Butcher of the

University of Florida, the company has made a conscientious effort to clean up. But the damage has been done.

Virulent bird flu has left the factories and moved into the farmyards of the poor, where it has had devastating effects. Poultry may represent a family's greatest wealth. The birds are often not eaten until they die of old age or illness. The cost of the virus to people who have raised birds for months or years is incalculable and the compensation risible: In Thailand, farmers have been offered one-third of their birds' value since the outbreak of bird flu.

Sometimes farmers who don't want to lose their investments illicitly trade their birds across borders. In Nigeria, virus-infected chickens threatened with culling are sold by the poor to even poorer people, who see nothing unusual in eating a sick or dead bird. So the birds—and the bird flu virus—slip away to other villages and other countries.

The Southeast Asian country without rampant bird flu is Laos, where 90% of poultry production is still in peasant hands, according to the U.S. Department of Agriculture. About 45 small outbreaks in or near commercial farms from January to March 2004 were quickly stamped out by culling birds from contaminated farms.

Migratory Birds Are Not the Problem

Some researchers still blame migratory birds for the relentless spread of the bird flu virus. But Martin Williams, a conservationist and bird expert in Hong Kong, contends that wild birds are more often victims than carriers. [In spring of 2005] for instance, about 5,000 wild birds died at Qinghai Lake in western China, probably from exposure to disease at commercial poultry farms in the region, according to Grain. The virus now in Turkey and Nigeria is essentially identical to the Qinghai strain.

Richard Thomas of Birdlife International, a global alliance of conservation organizations, and others dispute the idea that wild birds carried the flu virus from Qinghai to Russia and beyond. They point out that the disease spread from Qinghai to southern Siberia during the summer months when birds do not migrate, and that it moved east to west along railway lines, roads and international boundaries—not along migratory flyways.

What evidence there is for migratory birds as H5N1 carriers is contained in a study published in the Proceedings of the National Academy of Sciences. Researchers examined 13,115 wild birds and found asymptomatic bird flu in six ducks from China. Analysis showed that these ducks had been exposed earlier to less virulent strains of H5 and thus were partly immunized before they were infected with H5N1. On this slender basis, coupled with the fact that some domestic ducks infected for experimental purposes don't get sick, the study's authors contend that the findings "demonstrate that H5N1 viruses can be transmitted over long distances by migratory birds."

The commercial poultry industry, which caused the catastrophe in the first place, stands to benefit most.

Even so, the researchers conceded that the global poultry trade, much of which is illicit, plays a far larger role in spreading the virus. The Nigerian government traced its outbreak to the illegal importation of day-old chicks. Illegal trading in fighting cocks brought the virus from Thailand to Malaysia in fall 2005. And it is probable that H5N1 first spread from Qinghai to Russia and Kazakhstan last summer through the sale of contaminated poultry.

But an increasingly hysterical world targets migratory birds. In early February [2006], a flock of geese, too cold and tired to fly, rested on the frozen waters of the Danube Delta in Romania. A group of 15 men set upon them, tossed some into the air, tore off others' heads and used still-living birds as soccer balls. They said they did this because they feared the bird flu would enter their village through the geese. Many conservationists worry that what happened in Romania is a foreshadowing of the mass destruction of wild birds.

The Poor Are the Victims

Meanwhile, deadly H5N1 is washing up on the shores of Europe. Brown says the commercial poultry industry, which caused the catastrophe in the first place, stands to benefit most. The conglomerates will more and more dominate the poultry-rearing business. Some experts insist that will be better for us. Epidemiologist Michael Osterholm at the University of Minnesota, for instance, contends that the "single greatest risk to the amplification of the H5N1 virus, should it arrive in the U.S. through migratory birds, will be in free-range birds . . . often sold as a healthier food, which is a great ruse on the American public."

The truly great ruse is that industrial poultry farms are the best way to produce chickens—that Perdue Farms and Tyson Foods and Charoen Pokphand are keeping the world safe from backyard poultry and migratory birds. But what's going to be on our tables isn't the biggest problem. The real tragedy is what's happened in Asia to people who can't afford cheap, industrial chicken. And the real victims of industrially produced, lethal H5N1 have been wild birds, an ancient way of life and the poor of the Earth, for whom a backyard flock has always represented a measure of autonomy and a bulwark against starvation.

15

Department of Agriculture Is Protecting Consumers from Avian Influenza

Ron DeHaven

Ron DeHaven is the administrator of the Animal and Plant Health Inspection Service (APHIS), U.S. Department of Agriculture.

Note: The following article is excerpted from Ron DeHaven's testimony before the Committee on Agriculture, House of Representatives.

The U.S. Department of Agriculture (USDA) has made an extensive effort to protect consumers and the poultry industry from avian influenza, or AI, familiarly known as bird flu. Since the most dangerous strain of AI, H5NI, has never appeared in the United States, the USDA has implemented a number of programs to ensure that the virus is isolated and treated in countries where it has occurred. Americans can be assured that the government is responding to this threat with robust safeguards and detection methods. As long as poultry products are properly handled and cooked by consumers, there is little threat of the disease spreading to humans.

[Since mid-2005], a highly pathogenic strain of H5N1 avian influenza virus has been spreading across poultry populations in several Southeast Asian and Eastern European

Ron DeHaven, "Review of the Issues Related to the Prevention, Detection, and Eradication of Avian Influenza," Hearing Before the Committee on Agriculture, House of Representatives, One Hundred Ninth Congress, November 16, 2005. Reproduced by permission of Ron DeHaven.

countries. There have also been documented cases of the virus affecting humans who have been in direct contact with sick birds. There is worldwide concern that this H5N1 virus might mutate, cross the species barrier, and touch off a human influenza pandemic.

With this in mind, USDA's poultry health safeguarding programs are more important than ever, and we have bolstered our efforts across the board in response to the evolving disease threat overseas.

We also believe it is critical to effectively address the disease in poultry populations in the affected countries. Implementation of effective biosecurity measures, in concert with control and eradication programs, will go a long way towards reducing the amount of virus in these H5N1-affected countries, and thereby minimize the potential for this virus to spread to poultry in other areas of the world. These actions, if effectively implemented, would diminish the potential for a human influenza pandemic as well.

Avian influenza viruses found in birds do not pose any significant health risk to humans.

[In November 2005] I attended an international meeting on avian influenza, and I can report that there is widespread concern regarding this disease, as well as a strong commitment to work through international organizations to address the disease and improve the animal health infrastructure of countries in the region. That is why it is imperative that the United States remains engaged and shares resources and expertise with the officials in these countries.

Here in the United States, the National Strategy for Pandemic Influenza announced by President Bush on November 1 [2005] reflects the importance of these proactive measures on the animal health front. The President requested $91.35 million in emergency funds for USDA to further intensify its surveillance here at home, and to deliver increased assistance to countries impacted by the disease in hopes of preventing further spread of avian influenza.

With that introduction, I want to touch on a few more specific key points that I hope will help frame our discussion this morning. With regard to birds, avian influenza viruses are divided into two groups, low pathogenic avian influenza, or low path AI, and highly pathogenic, or high path AI. The highly pathogenic virus has typically produced far more severe clinical signs and higher mortality in birds than the lower pathogenic avian influenza viruses. Low path AI has been identified in the United States and around the world since the early 1900's. It is relatively common to detect low path, just as human flu viruses are a common finding in people; however, most avian influenza viruses found in birds do not pose any significant health risk to humans.

Security Measures Are Robust

Highly pathogenic AI has been found in poultry in the United States three times, in 1924, 1983, and 2004. The 1983 outbreak was the largest, ultimately resulting in the destruction of 17 million birds in Pennsylvania and Virginia before the virus was finally contained and eradicated. In contrast, the 2004 high path incident, it was in a flock of 6,600 birds in Texas. It was quickly found and eradicated. There were no significant human health implications or reports of human health problems in connection with any of these outbreaks.

In domestic poultry, the greatest concern has been infections with the H5 and H7 strains of the virus, which can either be highly pathogenic or low pathogenic. The low pathogenic H5 and H7 viruses are always of concern because they have shown a potential to mutate to the highly pathogenic form of the disease. Given these risks, safeguarding systems against avian influenza are robust and they are encompassing, among other things, trade restrictions on poultry and poultry products from overseas.

We have in place antismuggling programs; aggressive, targeted surveillance in commercial poultry operations and the live bird marketing system in the United States. We have cooperative efforts and information sharing with the States and the industry, and outreach to producers regarding the need for effective on-farm biosecurity measures.

Meat from the affected flocks would not enter the animal food or human food chains.

The USDA and our partners, including the Department of Interior, have also been looking for signs of avian influenza in wild birds in the United States, particularly in the Alaska migratory bird flyway, as we know these birds can serve as a reservoir for the disease.

Our ability to respond to a detection of avian influenza is designed to be just as robust as our safeguarding system. For highly pathogenic avian influenza, as well as for the low path strains of H5 and H7, APHIS [Animal and Plant Health Inspection Services] would work with States to quarantine affected premises, clean and disinfect those premises after the birds had been depopulated and disposed of. Positive highly pathogenic AI flocks would be depopulated, and meat from the affected flocks would not enter the animal food or human food chains. Surveillance testing would also be conducted in a quarantine zone in the surrounding area to ensure that the virus had been completely contained and eradicated.

On the trade front, there is an important new World Organization for Animal Health, or OIE, standard for avian influenza. This new standard obligates member countries to report any positive notifiable avian influenza test result. This notifiable avian influenza would include reporting all highly pathogenic strains of AI, as well as low pathogenic strains of

H5 and H7 subtypes detected in commercial poultry flocks. The OIE does not recommend trade restrictions for non-H5 or H7 low pathogenic strains of the virus.

The proper handling and cooking of poultry provides protection from all manner of viruses and bacteria, including avian influenza.

APHIS continues to work with its trading partners to promote the application of this new OIE standard. And in the event of any avian influenza outbreak, we would, of course, work to control and eradicate the disease, and also to demonstrate to trading partners that measures put in place were effective in controlling and eradicating the virus. APHIS would then urge trading partners to regionalize the United States for the disease, effectively allowing trade in poultry and poultry products to continue from unaffected areas.

Even though no human cases of avian influenza have been confirmed from eating properly prepared poultry, I would still like to end by reinforcing a few key food safety messages. . . . The proper handling and cooking of poultry provides protection from all manner of viruses and bacteria, including avian influenza. Important safety steps include washing hands, utensils and surfaces that have come in contact with raw poultry, fish and meats with warm soap and water. Avoid cross-contamination of other foods with raw meat, poultry and fish and their juices. And, of course, cook meat thoroughly and use a food thermometer. . . . Obviously, never consume raw or uncooked poultry or poultry products, and all meat products and other perishables should be refrigerated promptly after serving.

Organizations to Contact

American Farm Bureau Federation
600 Maryland Ave. SW, Suite 800, Washington, DC   20024
(202) 406-3600 • fax: (202) 406-3604
Web site: www.fb.org

The American Farm Bureau is an independent organization governed by and representing farm and ranch families for the purpose of analyzing their problems and formulating action to achieve educational improvement, economic opportunity, and social advancement. The organization publishes news, opinion articles, and online brochures available on its Web site.

American Farmland Trust
1200 18th St. NW, #800, Washington, DC   20036
(202) 331-7300 • fax: (202) 659-8339
e-mail: info@farmland.org
Web site: www.farmland.org

The American Farmland Trust encourages stewardship and conservation practices and works to win permanent protection for millions of acres of American farmland through publicly funded agricultural conservation easement programs. The organization publishes an e-newsletter along with research and policy papers concerning federal farm bills and other farm-related issues.

Farm Aid
11 Ward St., Suite 200, Somerville, MA   02143
(800) FARM-AID • fax: (617) 354-6992
e-mail: info@farmaid.org
Web site: www.FarmAid.org

Farm Aid was founded to help family farmers remain on their land in order to restore family farm-centered agriculture, which members believe ensures safe, healthful food, protects natural resources, and strengthens local economies. Farm Aid seeks to raise awareness of this mission, and funds, with an annual benefit music concert. The organization publishes a newsletter available through its Web site.

Farm Sanctuary

P.O. Box 150, Watkins Glen, NY   14891
(607) 583-2225 • fax: (607) 583-2041
e-mail: info@farmsanctuary.org
Web site: www.farmsanctuary.org

Farm Sanctuary was founded in 1986 to combat what it perceives as the abuses of industrialized farming and to encourage public awareness and activism about improved treatment of farm animals. Members document what Farm Sanctuary considers inhumane conditions at farms, stockyards, and slaughterhouses and conduct animal rescues. The organization produces several publications including the newsletter *Sanctuary News*, the teacher's guide *Cultivating Compassion*, booklets about farm animals such as *Life Behind Bars*, and research reports.

GRACE Factory Farm Project (GFFP)

215 Lexington Ave., Suite 1001, New York, NY   10011
(212) 726-9161 • fax: (212) 726-9160
e-mail: info@factoryfarm.org
Web site: www.factoryfarm.org

GFFP works to create a sustainable food production system that is healthy and humane, economically viable, and environmentally sound. The group works to help rural communities, family ranchers, and farmers around the country oppose the spread of new factory farms, and close down existing operations that adversely affect the health and well-being of communities. The organization publishes numerous reports about organic farming, agriculture's effects on the environment, and the treatment of farm animals.

Hudson Institute

1015 18th St. NW, Suite 300, Washington, DC 20036
(202) 223-7770 • fax: (202) 223-8537
e-mail: info@hudsondc.org
Web site: www.hudson.org

The Hudson Institute is a conservative think tank that supplies research analyses, books, and policy recommendations to leaders in communities, businesses, nonprofit organizations, and governments. The institute is committed to free markets and individual responsibility, confidence in the power of technology to assist progress, respect for the importance of culture and religion in human affairs, and measures that preserve and strengthen national security.

Humane Society of the United States (HSUS)

2100 L St. NW, Washington, DC 20037
(202) 452-1100
e-mail: www.hsus.org/contact_us/member_services.html
Web site: www.hsus.org

Established in 1954, currently with nearly 10 million members and constituents, HSUS is the nation's largest and most powerful animal protection organization, working in the United States and abroad to defend the interests of all animals. The group's major campaigns target four primary issues: 1) factory farming, 2) animal fighting and other forms of animal cruelty, 3) the fur trade, and 4) inhumane sport-hunting practices. The group publishes the quarterly newsletter *Wild Neighbors News*, the membership magazine *All Animals*, and an annual book series *The State of Animals*.

International Foundation for the Conservation of Natural Resources (IFCNR)

P.O. Box 1019, Poolesville, MD 20837
e-mail: info@ifcnr.com
Web site: http://biotech.ifcnr.com

The IFCNR is a global advocate of research and applied biotechnology. Members believe that biotechnology promises new ways to conquer disease and provide healthier, more robust crops while reducing the dangerous use of pesticides and the need to plow under wilderness acreage. The organization publishes opinion pieces, white papers about issues such as avian flu, and articles about the latest technological innovations in agriculture.

National Farmers Union (NFU)
5619 DTC Pkwy., Suite 300
Greenwood Village, CO 80111-3136
(800) 347-1961 • fax: (303) 771-1770
Web site: www.nfu.org

Officially called the Farmers Educational and Cooperative Union of America, the NFU is a general farm organization with a membership of nearly 250,000 farm and ranch families throughout the United States. NFU's primary goal is to sustain and strengthen family farm and ranch agriculture through legislative action at the local, state, and national levels. The group publishes a Web blog and an e-newsletter.

Organic Consumers Association
6771 South Silver Hill Dr., Finland, MN 55603
(218) 226-4164 • fax: (218) 353-7652
e-mail: www.organicconsumers.org/aboutus.htm#contact
Web site: www.organicconsumers.org

The OCA is an online nonprofit public-interest organization that promotes the views and advances the interests of the nation's estimated 50 million organic consumers. The OCA opposes industrial agriculture and genetic engineering and supports food safety, corporate accountability, fair trade policies, and environmental sustainability. The group publishes the newsletters *Organic Bytes*, *Biodemocracy News*, and *Organic View* in addition to opinion pieces and fact sheets.

Public Citizen
215 Pennsylvania Ave. SE, Washington, DC 20003
(202) 546-4996 • fax: (202) 547-7392

e-mail: cmep@citizen.org
Web site: www.citizen.org/cmep

Public Citizen is a national, nonprofit consumer advocacy organization founded in 1971 to represent consumer interests in Congress, the executive branch, and the courts. Public Citizen advocates openness and democratic accountability in government; consumers' right to seek redress in the courts; clean, safe, and sustainable energy sources; social and economic justice in trade policies; strong federal health, safety, and environmental protections; and safe, effective, and affordable prescription drugs and health care.

U.S. Department of Agriculture (USDA)
1400 Independence Ave. SW, Washington, DC   20250
(202) 720-3631
e-mail: agsec@usda.gov
Web site: www.usda.gov

The USDA is the cabinet-level federal department concerned with all agricultural issues in the United States. It administers the nation's food stamp, school meals, and infant nutrition programs; maintains 192 million acres of national forests and rangelands; is responsible for the safety of meat, poultry, and egg products; and helps ensure open markets for U.S. agricultural products and provides food aid to needy people overseas. The department publishes the *USDA Fact Book* and reports and fact sheets on hundreds of federal programs and research programs.

Bibliography

Books

Mark H. Bernstein — *Without a Tear: Our Tragic Relationship with Animals.* Urbana: University of Illinois Press, 2004.

Kenneth D. Black, ed. — *Environmental Impacts of Aquaculture.* Sheffield, UK: Sheffield Academic Press, 2001.

João Coimbra, ed. — *Modern Aquaculture in the Coastal Zone: Lessons and Opportunities.* Burke, VA: IOS, 2000.

Barry A. Costa-Pierce, ed. — *Ecological Aquaculture: The Evolution of the Blue Revolution.* Malden, MA: Blackwell Science, 2002.

Kathryn Marie Dudley — *Debt and Dispossession: Farm Loss in America's Heartland.* Chicago: University of Chicago Press, 2000.

Gail A. Eisnitz — *Slaughterhouse: The Shocking Story of Greed, Neglect, and Inhumane Treatment Inside the U.S. Meat Industry.* Amherst, NY: Prometheus, 1997.

Deborah Kay Fitzgerald — *Every Farm a Factory: The Industrial Ideal in American Agriculture.* New Haven, CT: Yale University Press, 2003.

Bruce L. Gardner   *American Agriculture in the Twentieth Century: How It Flourished and What It Cost.* Cambridge, MA: Harvard University Press, 2002.

Lorraine Garkovich, Janet L. Bokemeier, and Barbara Foote   *Harvest of Hope: Family Farming/ Farming Families.* Lexington: University Press of Kentucky, 1995.

Rick Halpern and Roger Horowitz   *Meatpackers: An Oral History of Black Packinghouse Workers and Their Struggle for Racial and Economic Equality.* New York: Twayne, 1996.

Roger Horowitz   *Putting Meat on the American Table: Taste, Technology, Transformation.* Baltimore: Johns Hopkins University Press, 2006.

T.V.R. Pillay   *Aquaculture and the Environment.* Malden, MA: Blackwell, 2004.

Matthew Scully   *Dominion: The Power of Man, the Suffering of Animals, and the Call to Mercy.* New York: St. Martin's, 2002.

Sally Shortall   *Women and Farming: Property and Power.* New York: St. Martin's, 1999.

Upton Sinclair   *The Jungle.* Tucson: See Sharp, 2003.

M. Suzanne Sontag   *Families on Small Farms: Case Studies in Human Ecology.* East Lansing: Michigan State University Press, 1996.

Selina M. Stead and Lindsay Laird, eds.	*Handbook of Salmon Farming.* New York: Springer, 2002.
Eric Thomas	*A Farm Through Time.* New York: Dorling Kindersley, 2001.
Stewart Emory Tolnay	*The Bottom Rung: African American Family Life on Southern Farms.* Urbana: University of Illinois Press, 1999.
Edwin Fuller Torrey	*Beasts of the Earth: Animals, Humans, and Disease.* New Brunswick, NJ: Rutgers University Press, 2005.

Periodicals

Josh Balk	"Stop Factory Farm Abuse," *Mother Earth News,* June/July 2005.
J. Patrick Boyle	"In Meatpacking, Progress to Be Proud Of," *Washington Post,* August 31, 2005.
Susan Bullers	"Environmental Stressors, Perceived Control, and Health: The Case of Residents Near Large-Scale Hog Farms in Eastern North Carolina," *Human Ecology: An Interdisciplinary Journal,* February 2005.
Brandon Copple	"Bovine Blues," *Forbes,* January 21, 2002.
David Elstein	"Recycling Feedlot Runoff," *Agricultural Research,* April 2003.

Kenneth Eng   "Environmental Pollution Requires Immediate Industry Attention," *Feedstuffs*, June 17, 2002.

Erica Gies   "Sustainable Seafood: All Fish Dishes Are Not Created Equal," *E*, November/December 2005.

Rich Heffern   "Farmers: Get Big or Get Out; Chronic Low Prices Force Families Off the Land as Agribusiness Grows," *National Catholic*, May 31, 2002.

Bette Hileman   "Guarding Against Mad Cow Disease: One Diseased Cow in Canada Sparks Calls for Stronger Regulations in the U.S.," *Chemical & Engineering News*, August 4, 2003.

Janet Kauffman   "The Fantasy of the Clip Art Farm: Notes from the New Rural Landscape," *Dissent*, Summer 2002.

Trent Loos   "Family Farmers Hijacked," *Feedstuffs*, May 9, 2005.

Jon R. Luoma   "Hogging the Air: The EPA Is Ready to Allow Factory Farms to Keep On Polluting," *Mother Jones*, July/August 2004.

Michael A. Mallin and Lawrence B. Cahoon   "Industrialized Animal Production—a Major Source of Nutrient and Microbial Pollution to Aquatic Ecosystems," *Population and Environment*, May 2003.

Robin Maynard   "Farming's Final Solution: Factory Farms and Mass Culls Are Unacceptable," *Ecologist*, April 2004.

Molly McDonough   "Down on the Farm: Laws Aimed at Boosting Family Famers May Violate Commerce Clause," *ABA Journal*, November 2003.

A.S. Monto   "The Threat of an Avian Influenza Pandemic," *New England Journal of Medicine*, January 27, 2005.

Danielle Nierenberg   "The Commercialization of Farming: Producing Meat for a Hungry World: Change 'Will Require a Rethinking of Our Relationship with Livestock and the Price We Are Willing to Pay for Safe, Sustainable, Humanely Raised Food,'" *USA Today*, January 2004.

Joel Novek   "Something Smells: Government Regulation Is Not Keeping Up with the Growth of Factory Hog Farms," *Alternatives Journal*, Fall 2003.

Tim O'Brien   "Factory Farming and Human Health," *Ecologist*, June 2001.

Susan S. Schiffman et al.   "Symptomatic Effects of Exposure to Diluted Air Sampled from a Swine Confinement Atmosphere on Healthy Human Subjects," *Environmental Health Perspectives*, May 2005.

Bob Schildgen   "Who Grows Your Food? And Why It Matters," *Sierra*, November/December 2004.

Index